Help Me! I'm a Religious Wreck and You Can Find Me in the Desert

A MUSTARD SEED READ

Tamara K. Kent

WestBow
PRESS
A DIVISION OF THOMAS NELSON

WestBow Press books may be ordered through booksellers or by contacting:

WestBow Press
A Division of Thomas Nelson
1663 Liberty Drive
Bloomington, IN 47403
www.westbowpress.com
1-(866) 928-1240

Because of the dynamic nature of the Internet, any Web addresses or links contained in this book may have changed since publication and may no longer be valid. The views expressed in this work are solely those of the author and do not necessarily reflect the views of the publisher, and the publisher hereby disclaims any responsibility for them.

ISBN: 978-1-4497-1086-6 (sc)
ISBN: 978-1-4497-1087-3 (dj)
ISBN: 978-1-4497-1085-9 (e)

Library of Congress Control Number: 2010943280

Printed in the United States of America

WestBow Press rev. date: 02/22/2011

A voice of one calling in the desert, "Prepare the way for the Lord, and make straight paths for him. Every valley shall be filled in, every mountain and hill made low. The crooked roads shall become straight, the rough ways smooth. And all mankind will see God's salvation" (Luke 3:4–6).

Contents

For my siblings in Christ
Butch, Guy, Gail, Penny, Baron, and Steve

Foreword

*F*aith and religion are often supposed to mean the same thing. However, any practice of religion without a heart of faith is merely religiosity. I would like to give a brief definition of terms referred to in this book. Our faith, religion, laws, church covenants, bylaws, doctrines, and religion can be sacred to us, but if we disconnect our practices from our personal relationship with God, we risk putting all our faith into the practice of our religion rather than in our living God. It is not the intention of this book to judge and criticize religion if it is practiced from the heart as a loving expression of faith. It is my intention to uplift the fallen who have stopped walking in their faith for reasons related to past religious performance or lack of support from their religion. In consideration of all, if our hearts are true, we will agree that religion without charity is never God's intention. Just as we could agree that faith without works is dead. Hope is the message of this book, hope that we will be able to cease from judging others and return to the practice of our faith with our hearts full of charity.

Faith is an internalized belief and trusting relationship in God our Father, Creator, and Savior, and we resolve to worship him in reverence for who he is. In contrast, religion without heartfelt faith is an externalized belief in a structure, or organization, but God may not be worshiped. In consideration of the message in this book, the old-fashioned acceptance that our faith and religion equate the same is not the way religion is viewed today. False religious practices often disregard faith.

Law, as mentioned in the Bible, refers to the Judaic law, which has three parts: the ceremonial law, civil law, and moral law.

Ceremonial law applies to worship, sacrifices, and festivals. Jesus fulfilled the law of sacrifice. God commanded the civil and moral laws to establish a relationship of love and respect between God and man. Jesus fulfilled the letter of the civil and moral law by maintaining his sincere love for God and others throughout his life. God called us to live by Jesus' example. Civil law is the law that applies to the cultures of the day and defines what is acceptable to daily life within the community. Love your neighbor as yourself is one premise of the civil code. The moral law reveals the nature of God. Moses gave us the moral law in the Ten Commandments. The moral law is a direct commandment from God and is binding and timeless.

Covenants, doctrines, and religiosity refer to peculiar, traditional beliefs each church organization uses to conduct its worship and other functions. Believers endanger their faith (relationship with God) by allowing outward practices of religion, church doctrine, covenants, and sacraments to supersede faith in relationship to God.

The intention of this book is to bring insight to issues that cause us to falter in our walk with God and help us weave through the maze of confusion we experience during a time of doubt and misunderstanding.

Preface

The physical desert is a fascinating place, but many of us have not lived in its barrenness. On the other hand, many have lived in a place of spiritual dryness and may be blessed to know that God also has a captivating plan for us in this. With our minds on God's use of the desert provided in the Bible, we may give awe to the spiritual significance of this wilderness. Remarkably, when perusing through the Old and New Testament, we find references to God's children who have undergone such a time of spiritual preparation in the desert. An amazing correlation exists between their reasons for going into solitude and God's unseen involvement during their separation from others. Most encouraging is the outcome when the person returns from the desert to advance spiritually in their walk of faith. Here we see evidence that God's Holy Spirit was both perfecting and protecting his will for their future.

Unbeknownst to the person, the situation taking place is part of the greater good God has planned for the ones he calls to serve him. For all purposes related to this book, when I speak of "being in the desert", it means to separate oneself for an indeterminate amount of time from the mainstream. It doesn't feel like an opportunity when we find our souls in this solitary place, or spiritual desert, but it does give us a chance to gain perspective. Trust me! A desert experience is part of a higher calling that God uses to redirect the awareness of His chosen.

It can prove to be an invaluable time and blessing in preparation for our future life and calling.

Four key things seem to prove true about this spiritual desert experience:

One: God makes the reservation for us in advance at a specific time and place in our faith journey where we can confront issues unhindered while trying to sort things out.

Two: God gives us the freedom to choose to take this route when he opens the door.

Three: God extends patience and grace in providing us the time and space needed to heal from tragedy, illness, our mistakes, or the mistakes of others.

Four: God desires to teach us personally, tailored lessons in the desert that will strengthen our faith and our relationship as we look to his word.

Bible characters acquainted with trials connected to their faith and calling experienced a time in the desert. Since they were all human, I would like to state emphatically that their uncertainty as to why they landed in the desert must have left them out of sorts, feeling like a *religious wreck*. The encouraging thing is that in each Biblical Desert Incident, the person of conviction, who met with religious confusion along the way got past the questioning of their faith and went on to fulfill their calling. Spending time in the desert became their response to a situation that had gotten out of their control. Whether they missed the mark through sin, misunderstood God's greater good, or faced opposition by sinful men, providence allowed them to find refuge in the desert.

Note clearly that in the scriptural account of Jesus, the Holy Spirit led him into the desert to battle with Satan, and because he was found without sin, he is able to remove our judgment. God understands the spiritual need of each individual and has a greater good in mind for our season in the desert. God still instructs this way today, protecting our calling and caring for us, even those of us who are *religious wrecks,* hiding out in our own spiritual desert.

Additionally, please note that unless otherwise indicated, the New International Version (NIV) was used for scriptural reference throughout the book.

Chart of Biblical Desert Incidents

BIBLICAL PERSONS	REASON FOR GOING TO DESERT	MIRACLE ACCOMPLISHED AS RESULT OF DESERT EXPERIENCE	SCRIPTURAL ACCOUNT REFERENCE
Jacob	Deceived Esau and stole the birthright; Fear of Esau	Jacob fathered the twelve tribes of Israel	Genesis 27:33–45
Hebrews (Israelites)	Exodus from Egypt to God's training ground for a holy nation	The Israelites became the Chosen People of God	Exodus 5 & 14 Numbers 5 & 14 Joshua 14
Moses	Killed an Egyptian soldier; Fear of Pharaoh	Led the Israelites out of Bondage; taught them how to serve God through the Ten Commandments	Exodus 2:11-3:22; 19 & 20
David	Evoked Jealousy in Saul; Fear of Saul	Became King of Judah in the lineage of Jesus Christ the Messiah	1Samuel 23:14-29 2Samuel 2:4, 5:3
Elijah	Prophet who challenged Baal; Fear of Jezebel	Proved that Baal worship was powerless and overthrew the priests of Baal	1Kings 19:1–17
John the Baptist	Seeking God's will by prayer and fasting; Fulfilling prophecy	Prepared hearts for the coming of Christ by teaching what repentance means. Confronted Pharisees and religious hypocrisy	Matthew 3:1–17 Luke 3:1–21
Jesus	Led by the Holy Spirit into the desert to be tempted by Satan	Restored the Kingdom of God on the earth; provided way of Salvation to man through redemption of sins; resurrected from physical death to share with us eternal life	Matthew 4: 1–11 Luke 4:1–13 John 3:16–21

Paul	Persecuting Christians; Learning about Jesus	Brought the gospel to the Gentiles and wrote a large portion of the New Testament	Acts 9:1–19 Galatians 1:15–22
Apostle John	Exiled to solitary life on Desert Island for Preaching Christ	Received book of Revelations; recorded End Time Prophecies to provide Truth, Hope, and Guidance for the Churches	Revelations 1:1–20:21

Introduction

The Hebrews spent a long time wandering the desert on the way to the Promised Land. No doubt that time of trials was a time of testing fraught with growing pains. Little did they appreciate that God was teaching them many truths about themselves and him. God was patiently molding a people to carry his name in a relationship with the Israelites. But his chosen people were not always quick students or patient followers in the school of faith. They complained and murmured about their hardships and placed the blame on Moses. They had no idea that God was trying to teach them how to walk by faith and overcome their circumstances.

Many of us respond to trials in the same negative spirit, showing God that we do not appreciate or understand them. But if we open our eyes to God's promises, there are extremely valuable lessons we can learn through our incident in the desert. This book is for helping us make sense out of the discouragement we often encounter in life on our way to the confidence that comes from a committed faith.

Whether you have been drifting in a spiritual wilderness for nine days, nine months, or nine years, *Help Me! I'm a Religious Wreck and You can Find me in the Desert* extends an oasis of hope to revive you from the heat. Its nine inspirational chapters are ready to provide you with insight and healing.

At a time when we turn back from what we once considered our calling, or others turn their back on us, the hard work of sifting through the disillusionment of a shipwrecked faith begins. As each chapter unfolds, we find the assurance that the circumstances in our dilemma may be for reproof or correction, or may simply be part of life's experiences. Either way, God's purpose is to nurture and grow our faith. Even if we reach the point where we abandon our belief system during our crisis, we can be sure that God does not abandon us.

God is with us to validate and comfort us with this truth; he knows where we are and where we have been. With stirring insight and a gentle course correction, this book opens our minds and hearts to the Word of God, to his wholeness, and to the completion of our salvation by grace and faith in Jesus.

1

A Day of Reckoning for Religion

We've all been there! On the day of our crisis when we needed faith the most, we couldn't find any. Not only is our faith failing, but we are also getting angry that after years of regular church attendance, in our hour of devastation, we are basically left standing alone. We don't get it! Our religion failed us, and now we are labeled "a religious wreck." To top it off, when no one comes alongside us in support, we feel bewildered and terribly hurt. We are for the moment a total basket case of blame and regrets. Where were the brethren in our hour of need? Perhaps it was awkward dealing with our concerns, a cause of discomfort, or an untimely inconvenience for others to realize we were wounded and in need of love and care. Did they move or did we? Or were we all too far from God? Nevertheless, a spiritual concussion hurts.

After our emotions calmed down, we found ourselves alone and rootless in the desert—not a physical desert but a spiritual desert. It is in this place that we discover the law of reaping and sowing. We may find we have sown and cultivated a deep religion and shallow relationships. Acting on the surface deception that all was well with our soul based on our church attendance, service, and offerings, we neglected to maintain a personal and faithful relationship with God.

1

As a result, we sit here broken in the desert, trying to figure out what went wrong. We are aggravated with the question, "Where were all our former Sunday associates when we were sitting there beaten?" Then reality dawns on us. Is it possible they weren't there for us because we were living with a religion coming between what should have been a family of believers?

Had we considered the possibility that religious ideations often come between us and our faith in Christ? The following reasoning might summarize our thought process nicely. In contrast to the life and teachings of Jesus, religiosity realistically reveals a reprehensible rudeness throughout its rule-based realm! Think about it! What happens to a body of believers when they become over-involved in the technicalities of outward religion and under-involved in faith? Has any religion with all of its externally attached peculiarities—you know, the significant dos and don'ts of our denomination—provided us with Jesus' example to live the way, the truth, and the life of faith we are called to as Christians?

The countless numbers of doctrinal practices we adhere to are insignificant if they are not truly born from a heartfelt expression of obedient, Bible-based faith. By honestly evaluating what we don't approve of, we may find that we are at times quoting Jesus' address to the Pharisees (see Matt. 23:23), acting like blind guides who strain out gnats (little issues) but swallow camels (big issues). If we let go of the peripherals and cut out the outward church standards we so often use to judge one another, we could touch more hearts. Simply stated, Christianity would be more successful if we put aside all our quirks and differences and upheld one common faith in the Lord as remarked in the words of an old cliche, *"And they will know we are Christians by our love."* Yes, they'll know we are Christians by our love!

The fact is, we spend the majority of our time defending our denominational lines and maintaining our right to practice the eccentricities that trademark our denomination. Worse still, something we really need to reckon with is how many of the mainline religions that claim the title Christian are walking in denominational arrogance. Where is our shared belief in one faith, one Lord, and one baptism? Imagine how beautiful the fellowship would be if Christians were done with living for Christ nominally and fell in love with Jesus with sincere hearts.

Jesus lived centered on the truth in his heart, instead of being dictated to by worldly minded religious leaders. Jesus saw all too clearly that their interpretations and six hundred addendums to the law had distorted the truth of God's word. God's people had lost their love for God and fell in love with their religious standing instead. They found their joy in their accumulated knowledge and a religious viewpoint that set them up to judge the shortcomings of others. Do we also adopt and excuse error in our theology when we allow judgment, based on the standards we hold, to become the primary focus of our faith? Have we become groups of modern-day Pharisees quickly swooping down on others in their sin, whamming them with the Bible and all that without any gentleness or concern? Or as the priests ignored the man beaten by thieves in the parable of the Good Samaritan, do we leave those overcome by Satan to perish in their wounded spiritual condition? Are we not called to love and to restore one another to faith in God's goodness and mercy. Are we doing that?

> Jesus replied, And you experts in the law, woe to you, because you load people down with burdens they can hardly carry, and you yourselves will not lift one finger to help them (Luke 11:46).

So now, can we say that we are very grateful for the crisis that helped us stop being religious? Jesus practiced a new kind of faith. His faith and ministry came from his relationship with the Father and the Holy Spirit, and he didn't go around verbally slapping facts from the written code to condemn people like those scribes, Pharisees, and teachers. He didn't have impure motivations to put himself up by putting others down through his knowledge of the law. Jesus fulfilled the law. He is the word of God made flesh. His parables and miracles exercised through his love, not his degrees of study, showed how much could be achieved in reconciling people to place their trust in God.

He was such a revolutionary to take a stand in opposition to the rule-based religion of the day. How disconcerting it must have been for the Pharisees to see Jesus place his attention on individuals while disregarding the traditions and laws of their religion. Shouldn't our aim be to become like Jesus in his loving treatment of people with respect to their personal physical and spiritual needs? Shouldn't we separate our faith from the religious mindset that ignores individuals and promotes group thinking? Jesus' gentle treatment of souls, with disregard for the rules, worked a lot more effectively in leading people to repentance and true faith in God than any former judgmental warnings. Jesus made disciples who were men after God's own heart. The religious leaders made followers who were living by rules and not in relationships. Religion, misused, is both impersonal and cold hearted. I am sorrowful to remember the years of my life I wasted to promote religion and take pride in its programs, instead of raising up Christ.

I knew it was time for me to make a radical change in my life's philosophy, and it might be time for all of us to make a change regarding our representation of Christianity to the world. It is definitely past time to curb our differences and work on promoting peace among us. As we know, that is something that starts on a personal basis from within each of our hearts. Admitting we are, at times, more religious than faithful is the first step. It might actually be therapeutic for the true disciples to get angry over the ruckus that false religious misrepresentations of the gospel are causing. We should take a stand together in love and truth and reclaim Christianity for what it is. As Christians, we have the most powerful and peaceful faith on earth, but because of our religious conjecture, we have lost our witness to the world. If we do not demonstrate a harmonious faith, how can we expect to move the world in the right direction?

When was the last time you attended a service where the Holy Spirit was so present in ministry that all hearts there were united in a spirit of unquestioned love for God and one another? That kind of fellowship should be the rule, not the exception, every time Christians gather. The trouble we have gotten ourselves into has its origin in our embracing the lies of a religious ideology. We lose the purpose for the gospel when we take the ideas of our particular branch of Christianity and call that our faith. We preach our dos and don'ts but fail to teach others to live by love, which is the true expression of the faith of Christ. Furthermore, we are losing our youth with church functions that are not based on the teachings of Jesus. We are handing down a culture of church-based religion, not faith-based Christianity. Even the names of our churches often indicate areas where we are stuck in our theology. Just suffice it to say there is a big chasm between our traditional divisions and the foundational brotherhood of our faith in Jesus. Putting the rock-solid words of Jesus into practice is the bottom line for our entire spiritual ministry. We just cannot stand united if we let our religious cultures replace faith. Jesus is not only our personal Savior, but He is also our Lord. We need to serve Him, not a sect or a divisive group religion.

I am hopeful that all Christians would separate their faith, the desire in their hearts for God, from the practice of a religion they do not clearly understand. I am writing to Christians who need to be reminded that looking to Jesus will help any soul who needs discernment to separate the bogus from the truth in regard to their belief system. What doesn't matter should not matter. In God's economy, it's not a man's religion that matters; it's what's in his heart about Jesus. Faith in Jesus is what God desires to find as the foundation of our religious conviction. Here is where we should offer our gratitude for the many interdenominational Bible studies that do a great work in bringing the body together to study and grow as one focused on the Word of God.

We need to realize, like those who humbly participate in interdenominational gatherings, that the pride we feel for our particular religious label has no value in getting us closer to God. The Lord looks at our heart, not at our label. Placing our faith and trust in Jesus is the only key to eternal life. As Christians, we believe that there is not a religious practice or tradition on earth that has the power to offer us what Jesus has already given us. Nevertheless, we need to look honestly at what we are doing with our testimony of Christianity.

Religious ideas and traditions that take precedence over Jesus' words or divide us with piece parts of the gospel miss God. Please do not worry about losing your religion. If you fill up on religion, you will not have any room in your heart for faith.

Religious ideas, or traditional belief systems that hand down rituals from generation to generation, wherein the receiving generation has no understanding of the significance of the ritual, are the hallmark standards of a manmade religion. We may have a denomination founded on the Apostle's Creed, but men in the business of religion have taken us off course. One person discovers some piece of wisdom and says we should believe this and do it this way. Another man comes along and says we should believe that and do it that way. *In the same way that manmade changes have replaced this with that, religion replaces faith in God with trust in religion.*

Please stop and understand there is a difference between observing sacramental laws and rituals just for the sake of religious duty and in having a faithful relationship with God through following Jesus. The former reveres God in the name of religion, and the latter reveres God through faith in the name above all names. Our religion and our faith should be one in expressing the love we have for God. Our worship of God from a pure heart in spirit and in truth will open doors to ministry. Disconnected hearts performing external rituals of a church service will close doors to ministry.

Religious gatherings that are void of the spirit and disregard the truth can become a mundane script someone else has written for us to act out. There is a difference between following a religious paper trail and in believing in the miraculous salvation offered to us through our faith. Jesus' relationship with us supersedes all the laws scripted by man. He taught us to have faith in God, not a religion about God. Which has the greater authority, religion designed by man or faith given to us by Jesus? Jesus said that all authority (Matt 28:18) in heaven and on earth had been placed into his hands (John 3:35) by the Father. So we can be sure holding onto religion is not the way. Religion does not relate; it rules. Faith, placed in Jesus' hands, is our bedrock.

Religious leaders are imperfect men who have the capacity to behave wrongly through self-centered and self-appointed means. Therefore, it is important that we are well-grounded in the word of God since our leaders are capable of promoting ideologies that can separate us from the love of God. When a religious leader usurps authority in the name of God, he is free to rule over men's spirituality through deception. Furthermore, men who do not cherish the gift of life itself dishonor God. Any man who claims to be religious, but who does not give especial care to loving and respecting the people on this planet as equal recipients of the freedom and blessing of life, is not a godly man. Goodness expresses itself in kindness, whereas evil expresses itself in cruelty. How blessed we are that God sent Jesus.

Traditionally we have seen the moral of the religious story play out when one man sets up a religion, to set one man up, to cast another man down. We call that the built-in-trap-system of religion. Not so in Jesus' example of faith. In his role as our savior, he set himself up on a cross, to establish a faith to lift us up. *Jesus restored our hearts to God, to lift us up in faith, to keep us from being cast down in the trap of sin.*

Jesus is the originator of our Christian faith, and our lifestyle as a whole should be a cohesive representation of him. We should align ourselves with Jesus, who manifested the love of God as a human being. He was not in the business of religion. By faith, he sought daily guidance from the Holy Spirit and lived according to God's will in loving us. Contrast Jesus' peaceful love of others, where Jesus lays down his life, without harming anyone around him in the process, and place that beside hateful, selfish, and bigoted acts of religion. Jesus lays down his life through his sacrificial death on the cross to offer us eternal life, while others use their religion as a way to obtain eternal life.

The soul entrusted to Jesus brings us eternal life with salvation, peace, and a hopeful joy. The religious soul without the Holy Spirit brings us condemnation, depression, and sorrow. *Just simply realize that God wants to wipe out sin from the planet, and he uses his love, manifested through the humble life of Jesus, to do it.* Performing religious rituals will not wipe out sin from our planet nor earn you a place in heaven. Jesus showed us the Father's will and instructed us that we should love one another as he loved us. He was not acting on some deceptive religious ideology to gain something for himself in eternity. He simply placed his life fully into the Father's will and lived according to the guidance of the indwelling Holy Spirit. Jesus met and loved people right where they were and offered to help each one individually as needed.

Christ's death on the cross is in fulfillment of the prophecies that said the Lamb of God would sacrifice his life to buy ours back from sin. Jesus died at the hands of sinful men, first because he is our Savior, but also to give us a picture of what sinfulness, left unchecked in this world, can do. Sinful acts, such as lying, stealing, killing, and destroying the innocent are serious enemies. Jesus conquered the power of our sin when he was crucified on our behalf. But that's not the entire gospel … we have to go beyond the crucifix. The gospel does not end with Jesus' death on the cross.

The fact that Jesus came back to life through the resurrection and sent us the Holy Spirit completes the gospel in its fullness. We are born again when we trust in Jesus, repent from our sins, and receive the Holy Spirit. After our conversion we have the ability to live as Jesus did in a relationship of faith and trust in our Heavenly Father. *By placing the Holy Spirit in Jesus from conception, God wanted to show mankind that He has provided a way out of the futility of a life marred by sin's sorrow. The Spirit of Truth sent to us by Jesus enables us to share the same gift of life that overcomes sin and death through the indwelling Holy Spirit.*

> And I will ask the Father and he will give you another counselor to be with you forever—the Spirit of Truth. The world cannot accept him, because it neither sees him nor knows him. But you know him, for *he* lives with you and *will be in you* (John 14:16–17).

> But when the Spirit of Truth comes he will guide you into all truth. He will not speak on his own; he

> will only speak what he hears, and he will tell you
> what is yet to come (John 16:13).

In contrast to Christ's sacrifice, our relentless pursuit of religion with its focus on our manmade programs and our pride for all our good works appears to be religious idolatry. Think again about this statement: *Religion rules, but faith relates.* Religion, apart from Christ, compels us to observe its rules through carnal means, such as pulling one up by one's bootstraps. But what are we doing to deny our sin? Is our self-sacrificing service honorable? Are we picking up our cross to express our faith, or just upholding tradition? Faith and obedience to the message of the gospel will motivate us to honor God and serve others out of the love that flows from our relationship to the indwelling Holy Spirit.

> Jesus said, "If you love me you will obey what I
> command. This is my commandment that you love
> one another" (John 14:15).

The real vulnerability we have as church members is that we spend all our energy on religion itself and do not obey the simplicity of Jesus' command to love one another. We make divisions amongst ourselves based on our labor for the church when such labor may be done more from a prideful attitude than from a gentle servant's heart. Is the measure for our Christianity in relationship to our church functions or in our relationship to God?

Moreover, the Holy Spirit is not of the worldly secular system, nor is it affiliated with the strands of earthly wisdom men have pieced together from traditional practices or the business of religion handed down through the ages. No, the Holy Spirit embodies the love of God in purity, and he will keep us from sinning. He offers love to others transparently and kindly through our relationship to him and his relationship with our heavenly Father. The works that we do and the fruit that we bear as the body of Christ, the family of God, is to be in obedient and joyful response to the Holy Spirit.

We simply cannot flesh it out, no matter how superior a hold we have on religion or how ingrained our denial is of the world's fascination with religiosity. We cannot make it without submitting to his Holy Spirit, the Spirit ushered into the world through Jesus birth and entrusted to us in his resurrection. Our freedom to live in love comes to us from the same Holy Spirit to whom Jesus yielded and allowed to guide him through his humanity. This is how Jesus by faith was able to choose to love and not to sin. Jesus kept pure by staying in relationship to the Father's will through the indwelling Holy Spirit with him from the moment of his conception. The same opportunity to walk in freedom from religious edicts and laws is ours through the gift of the Spirit of Truth, who is with us and lives in us. Acceptance of Jesus' humanity and divinity is the bedrock of our faith. God imparted his divine nature in the person of the Holy Spirit to counsel Jesus. Knowing this, it makes sense that he will do the same for us when we are baptized and born again through faith.

God's spirit was alive in Jesus as the companion of Jesus, and that spirit of love and holiness kept Jesus in the Father's will. *He lived to demonstrate what restored humanity—humanity set free from sin's effect—could do for the people on this planet.* We cannot think that we only need a religion, creed, or doctrine to become Christ like. We first of all need to reconnect with God's original plan through the Savior, who opened the gate. Our Savior imparted to us a faith that grows through the grace of humility. We are not to be servants to any prideful, empty religion. Gaze clearly into these words of Jesus regarding the religious leaders of the day. You will see that he took on those empty parts of the philosophy of religiosity exposing it for the vain attempt it was to appease God. Religious malpractice and religion misused may be an attempt by man to make him appear righteous, and thereby deceive himself into thinking he is godly. Regardless of its motivation, promoting a religion to the exclusion of faith in Christ shows that one clearly misunderstands our Heavenly Father. *When Jesus brought the kingdom of heaven to earth, he exposed religion for its self-centered patterns and replaced it with other-centered faith.*

"Be careful," Jesus warned them. "Watch out for the yeast of the Pharisees and that of Herod" (Mark 8:15).

And when you pray, do not be like the hypocrites, for they love to pray standing in the synagogues and on the street corners to be seen by men (Matt 6:5).

Be careful not to do your "acts of righteousness" before men, to be seen by them. So when you give to the needy, do not announce it with trumpets, as the hypocrites do in the synagogues and on the streets, to be honored by men (Matt 6:1–2).

You hypocrites! Isaiah was right when he prophesied about you: "These people honor me with their lips, but their hearts are far from me. They worship me in vain; their teachings are but rules taught by men" (Matt 15:7–9).

Woe to you, teachers of the law and Pharisees, you hypocrites! You give a tenth of your spices—mint, dill, and cumin. But you have neglected the more important matters of the law-justice, mercy and faithfulness. You should have practiced the latter, without neglecting the former. You blind guides! You strain out a gnat but swallow a camel.

Woe to you, teachers of the law and Pharisees, you hypocrites! You clean the outside of the cup and dish, but inside they are full of greed and self-indulgence. Blind Pharisee! First clean the inside of the cup and dish, and then the outside also will be clean.

Woe to you, teachers of the law and Pharisees, you hypocrites! You are like whitewashed tombs, which looks beautiful on the outside but on the inside are full of dead men's bones and everything unclean. In the same way, on the outside you appear to people as righteous but on the inside you are full of hypocrisy and wickedness (Matt 23:23–28).

Today, just like the scribes and Pharisees of old, man makes his attempts to reach God, to be like God, and to make himself God-like through the tenets of religious belief and sacraments. All deeds of religion done without sincere reverence for God and love for others are actions that begin and end in woe. We must not be those whose duties are merely acts of men before men. Practices that do not show appreciation for God's love and respect for others often have little to do with purity, faithfulness, mercy, love, or justice. There is no way to the Father except through Jesus, and there is no work with eternal benefit, apart from Jesus. Still, man thinks he is pleasing God and being loving when he performs his religious duties to gain recognition. Men who do not consider what Jesus had to say about religious works could at least consider the love of God, which was the foundational basis for all Jesus shared in his miracles and parables.

Jesus, who was God incarnate, brought the love of God into this world in human form. It was the Holy Spirit of God at work in Jesus, which allows his followers to feel God's tender concern and grasp the true meaning of love. God is love.

In case you hadn't noticed, living without love makes our religion a not-so-humble proposition. Sometimes, organized religion seems to place an undue emphasis on appearing righteous and holy. Many of our world's religions have designed a whole set of plans that one can follow to achieve "holiness." Being an end unto itself, religion is man's goal for man, not God's goal for man. Having an appearance of holiness is not the goal one should wish to attain. *Living in love and unity, as well as providing service, respect, and honoring one another leads us to live holy lives.* However, the actual "state of holiness" itself is a byproduct of the indwelling Holy Spirit at work in our lives. Only God can claim holiness. To be sure, we should strive to live separate, holy lives. By holy, I mean living in opposition to the false religious, worldly, or carnal mindset. Even in that, we need to understand that our attempts to live pleasing and holy lives before God will not result in our attaining the fullness of God's purity in this lifetime.

Our focus should not be on achieving anything for promoting ourselves but should be on loving God. Through our faith and trust in the Holy Spirit, we give him access to our entire heart, mind, and soul, and that access is not through any religion. Religion is a poor substitute for a relationship with God.

The following scripture shows us the kind of loving work God wants us to do in his name. Notice there are no religious sacraments or ordinances advocated in the following passage:

> Then the King will say to those on his right, "Come, you who are blessed by my Father; take your inheritance, the kingdom prepared for you since the creation of the world. For I was hungry, and you gave me something to eat, I was thirsty, and you gave me something to drink. I was a stranger and you invited me in. I needed clothes and you clothed me, I was sick and you looked after me, I was in prison and you came to visit me." Then the righteous will answer him, "Lord, when did we see you hungry and feed you, or thirsty and give you something to drink? When did we see you a stranger and invited you in, or needing clothes and clothe you? When did we see you sick or in prison and go to visit you?" The King will reply, "I tell you the truth, whatever you did for one of the least of these brothers of mine, you did for me."
>
> Then he will say to those on his left, "Depart from me, you who are cursed, into the eternal fire prepared for the devil and his angels. For I was hungry, and you gave me nothing to eat. I was thirsty and you gave me nothing to drink. I was a stranger and you did not invite me in. I needed clothes and you did not clothe me, I was sick and in prison and you did not look after me." They will answer, "Lord, when did we see you hungry or thirsty or a stranger or needing clothes or sick or in prison, and did not help you?" He will reply, "I tell you the truth, whatever you did not do for one of the least of these, you did not do for me." Then they will go away to

eternal punishment, but the righteous to eternal life
(Matthew 25:34-46).

Elevating religious rituals apart from faith and love, while failing
to exhibit acts of mercy and charity becomes our misdirected attempt
to earn our way into God's grace. Instead, we are to take care to share
God's grace to fulfill the needs of God's children. When we fail to
heed Jesus' warning to care for others, we are guilty of attaching a
false belief system to our faith by basing our standing before God
solely on our outward religious image. The truth is salvation is a gift
from God that we receive through grace (Ephesians 2:8). We cannot
do anything to earn or elevate ourselves in God's sight. Jesus is the
only way to the Father, and as we give our lives to him, we receive
our salvation in exchange. Those who receive this gift of salvation
find that God's love becomes the inner motivation for the love we
shower on others. We receive and give through the grace of faith,
not the outward works of religion.

Here is where we should concentrate our faith. This is the
bottom-line basis for our Christianity. Everything we do for God
must be done through Jesus, not just as a result of our religion. His
way leads us to do the Father's will.

> Jesus answered, "I am the way and the truth and
> the life. No one comes to the Father except through
> me" (John 14:6).

We can't put our professions of love before God and declare
ourselves to be godly if we do nothing to show our love for others.
That is the futile attempt of man to expect that God will honor and
elevate us for our profession of religion and obedience to perform the
works of the church. *Faith in Jesus is the key to a relationship with the
Father. A man's nominal religion is not the key to anything; rather it is
often the lock on the door, which no man is ever able to open.*

2

Reconciliation, or "Wreck of Conciliation," by Religion

efore we address the subject at hand, we should first consider what the words reconciliation and conciliation mean from a biblical perspective. Reconciliation means reestablishing relationship. Conciliation means to bring into a peaceful agreement. Jesus' life and death is the reconciliation between God and man. As a result of Jesus' conciliation, we can now live in a secure relationship of agreement and peace with God.

> For if when we were God's enemies, we were reconciled to him through the death of his Son, how much more, having been reconciled, shall we be saved through his life! Not only is this so, but we also rejoice in God through our Lord Jesus Christ, through whom we have now received reconciliation (Romans 5:10–11).

Furthermore, the ministry we have chosen as his followers is a ministry of reconciliation.

> All this is from God, who reconciled us to himself through Christ and gave us the ministry of reconciliation: that God was reconciling the world to himself in Christ, not counting men's sins against them. And he has committed to us the message of reconciliation (2Corinthians 5:18–19).

It is so important to God that we maintain our efforts of conciliation with all that Jesus tells us to be reconciled to our brother before we offer our prayers to God at the altar. Sometimes, we rush straight into our religious meetings not caring that we have broken relationships with others. Living by faith shows us that we must be at peace with others in order to offer our gifts to God. This also means that offering our spiritual gifts in service requires us to be in a conciliatory relationship with God and others.

> Therefore, if you are offering your gift at the altar and there remember that your brother has something against you, leave your gift there in front of the altar. First go and be reconciled to your brother; then come and offer your gift (Matt 5:23–24).

Anyone who has failed to find credence in the fact that we must not let our religion overrule our faith or it must be reckoned with has already branded me a heretic. But the message in this book is not heretical, nor is it a slam against religion or religious persons. It is rather an appropriate voice to address the true heresy that has taken the gospel captive and has turned it into a joint religious venture. The fact is many of our churches labeled as Christian churches are in reality- fully staffed- companies involved in a religious business venture. There I said it, and I'll say this next. It is time to ask ourselves an appropriate question. Why on earth do we believe that our chosen religious bent, which we work to straighten out weekly in our church company, is more important than our faith in Christ? If that is heretical on my part, bear in mind that not all of the heretical ideas of ages past have been untrue. Major strides have been made by Christians referenced as heretics to lead people back to saner, more truthful realities of God and how we relate to him. Anyway, I am not here as a heretic or to speak for myself. I am not writing to propose that I have any superior knowledge or new revelation. I do not. Just bear with me and decide if you too will agree that there is no one-size-fits-all religion as each religion claims, but there is a one-way-saves-all faith in Jesus Christ. And we, as Christians, are called to reconcile others to the facts concerning the gospel of Christ whose redemption leads us to become one family of believers. Yet, we still insist on building a religious market on every corner.

We are not right in our saying that churches and religious organizations in themselves are bad. No one can refute the millions of souls saved and the charitable acts that span the globe. However, religious organizations have, at times, taken the good news of the gospel away from man, discoloring it to meet their standard brands. Everywhere you look, there are souls needing a shelter from past stormy experiences inside religious institutions, and hearts hungry for freedom from the oppressive wreckage caused by various religious organizations. Instituted religion and the men in charge have historically created confusion with authoritative misrepresentations of God. Power has gone to the head of many religious leaders and church members, who through pride have misused their places of authority to represent our Father, the creator of humanity. Arrogance has wounded seekers, created bitterness, and caused many to despair of the true place God wishes to have in our lives. A little insight into these matters explains why so many believers are in the spiritual desert.

The personal storms caused by the wreck of conciliation by false leaders, apostles, and prophets lording over the believers caught up in their religious folly have caused the most humble and honest souls to flee from churchgoing and abandon fellowships altogether. False prophecies and teachings still aid daily to the demise of many who listen to and embrace distortions of the truth. They tell people what they want to hear concerning health and wealth and God's unfathomable grace. Unfortunately, what they fail to tell us is that God will not tolerate sin or greed. Not to mention there are more blatant sins we or others have experienced through professing believers. Jesus warned us that in the last days, many would turn from the faith, and it is safe to say we are currently experiencing a famine of the truth. Being forewarned should make us want to get back to our true faith in the gospel of Jesus Christ as quickly as possible.

> At that time many will turn away from the faith
> and will betray and hate each other, and many false
> prophets will appear and deceive many people.
> Because of the increase of wickedness, the love of
> most will grow cold, but he who stands firm to the
> end will be saved (Mathew 24:10–13).

No doubt about that. The hands of sinful men have made a wreck out of religion. Nevertheless, we must stand firm and keep a pure heart. We cannot place the blame on Jesus, or our Father in Heaven. *We need a change in our mindset that recognizes there is a difference between a falsely twisted religion and a truly straight-and-narrow road of faith.*

Take heart if you are one of the souls temporarily living outside of houses or organizations of worship. It is the goal of this book to help us return to fellowship with people of likeminded faith. There is a true reconciliation; the original foundation is that all men who worship God need to come together finally on this one basic fact: God gave us love. We know it, feel it, and have lived with it all the days of our lives. God has revealed himself as a loving God. Humanity has wrecked his image using religious judgment and condemnation to invoke fear of God as the means for coming to him. It is true that God doesn't accept sin in our relationship with him, but Jesus has made atonement for sin.

We cannot love God with religious attempts or religiosity to create reconciliation between God and us. Trying to get to God through a pious religion is not the same as going to God through faith in Christ. Misuse of religion has managed to cause a "wreck of conciliation," leaving men confused, abandoned, and still stuck in sin. Men then think that they are justified from their sin by pointing the blame and guilt on the confusion caused by the religions around them. In contrast, our *reconciliation* through Jesus Christ atones for guilt, removes the finger pointing, and enables us to serve God from the actual love of God and his gift of faith. None of that is attributable to any religious practice on our part.

Say this with me. God is love. His commandments given in his word are wisdom to protect us from the ravages of wrongdoing. All wrongdoing is sin. There are moral absolutes, which we honestly, as caring, civil human beings, regardless of the differences from which we base our beliefs, must uphold. This is a truth necessary for maintaining a stable civilization. Our love of God, with acceptance and obedience to the Ten Commandments, are the foundational moral absolutes that bring blessings to us. Devotion to uphold these ten moral absolutes recorded in Deuteronomy 5 will not cause the separation of souls, but will bring us into one accord because they are the standard truths for the harmony of our Christian faith.

Although I am writing to Christians, I want us to realize that other souls do join us in confusing their religious expression for the faith in their hearts. *The two expressions—religion and faith—are not one in the same thing.* Religion is an external structure which can be used as an outward expression of our faith. Faith is an internal relationship with God. Faith expresses itself from the love of God, who indwells our soul. Religiosity is a distortion of both of these truths. We must be sure that we are not using religion or following a religious leader as the only basis for our relationship to God. Our religion cannot define or dictate the faith that comes from a personal relationship with our Savior. Worship of the Father in heaven, in spirit and in truth, will move our hearts to have love and compassion for all. Worship in the presence of ungodliness through religion will move the soul to hold hate and contempt of others in our hearts. We have witnessed this in historical tragedies caused by men who misused the name of God in war, acts of terror, and violence.

After having said this, we would do well to do the research necessary to see how our religion incorporates its training programs and sacred words into its practices. The sacred word for Christians is the Bible, and adherence to its teachings protects us from the sin within ourselves that would sin against our fellows. Do we even understand the significance of or the meaning behind our religious observations? Take this to heart. Has our adherence to our religious practices reconciled us to God? Alternatively, have we allowed it to replace and thus make a wreck out of our heartfelt faith? Have we found Jesus' reconciliation, or felt the sting of religious wreck of conciliation? *We must honestly answer the question, Do we enjoy our religion as a gift, or do we endure it? Faith in Jesus gives us freedom.*

Who is the founder of our belief system or denomination? Is there anything in his revelation that compares to the example that Jesus gave of love and service to God and others? It's that simple. You cannot ignore the greatest teacher who came to be the Savior of humanity. How can you be sure, without taking the time to study the example of Christ for yourself? In addition, if you stop to realize just what your faith professes, then it is imperative that you remain openhearted and open-minded toward the belief systems in which other souls, apart from Christ and the true gospel, feel turmoil. God set us free in Christ. Jesus came to show us the way to live by his spirit indwelling us with love and truth. Who else has brought such power into the lives of men? Who else has offered such peace? Who else has offered such a freeing salvation for our souls? Who else taught us by example to keep our inward and outward lives completely aligned? We cannot be false outwardly and deny what we believe to be true inwardly. Our faith in Christ makes us desire purity. The truth and love he offers is not duplicitous; it is genuine. We cannot wear our outward Christianity and inwardly excuse our misbehavior and bad attitudes, or we will be living like whitewashed tombs.

We may not be able to fully acknowledge Jesus because we have confused him with the error of the false religious groups that have characterized themselves as Christian but instead have brought wreck-conciliation upon the world. Their professions have opposed the reconciliation God meant for us to have in his only begotten son Jesus Christ. Nevertheless, this cannot continue to be an excuse for us. We cannot look at others and turn our backs on Christ. We must look at Christ and put our focus on his words and his example in scripture. *Be sure of this one thing: no one is free to stop searching until the search has set you free.*

Is our faith in the God who loves us with an everlasting love in Christ, or do we have a fearful expectation of the God of everlasting judgment? The answer to those two questions tells you whether the gospel message you have received comes from the reconciliation of Jesus Christ or from the wreck of conciliation from the preaching of a different and false gospel. We know that God will hear us when we pray to stay in his will and to be delivered from evil. True worshipers who seek God in his spirit of truth will receive God's gifts of peace, joy, and freedom from the bondages of false religions' deceptions.

When we are true to God, we will not pick up attitudes of a self-righteous pride. We will avoid falling for false doctrines that make us think we will only progress if we perform some religious act. The truth sets us free from the entanglement of selfish thinking, including the thinking that observing religious rituals themselves will make us more acceptable or more pleasing to God. Religious practices of worship, creeds based on giving, revelations, or powers of a denomination based on its wealth and size do not necessarily prove that they are signs of God's blessing.

On the other hand, we are not to consider personal hardships or persecutions as signs of God's curse or punishment for our sin. Much of those teachings allow us to judge ourselves better than others and cause us to have a self-righteous pride. That sort of pride means that we definitely are distorting the truth, which is that Jesus Christ is the reconciliation between God and us. This is all the blessing we need. When we look at our blessings or troubles as signs of God's approval or disapproval, we are on the wrong path. Jesus warned us that adulterous generations will seek after signs (Matt 12:39). Recall also that when Satan tempted Jesus in the wilderness, he promised Jesus all the riches in the world if Jesus would just bow down and worship Satan. If you have all the riches in the world, but still have impurity in your life, you might want to ask yourself where all your wealth came from. Nothing apart from Jesus' sacrifice and his teachings can put us on the right path to God. Jesus is the way to the Father, and we should not let any doubtful disputations lead us astray. We are not to follow after signs and blessings.

> Jesus said, "Blessed rather are those who hear the word of God and obey it" (Luke 11:28).

Furthermore, when we attend church, is our focus first on going to honor and bless God, or are we attending worship services mainly to implore God to bless us? When we hold onto our faith in Christ, we can keep a pure heart in the observance of sacraments both individually and corporately, but let us not attribute this to our doctrines. When we worship with our spirit and in truth, we make honoring God an expression of our faith, not an expression of our religion. Jesus is the firstborn of all true worshippers.

In examining the truth of the way Jesus honored the Father in a parent/child fellowship, we can live in the same security as heirs in Christ. From our new nature as God's children, we have freedom to give respect and honor to God as we worship. In return, we receive his direction in our lives. *Life is a gift, and the human experience, without bondage to our sin nature, in perfect fellowship with our Creator Father, is the most blessed reality we will ever experience.* God is a present helper, a friend for refuge, and he is interested in us, just as we are interested in loving and peaceful relationships with the people we love. He invites us to fellowship with him through faith and daily communion of our hearts with his. It's time for us on Earth to use this revelation of faith and revitalize the way we worship.

> Jesus said, "Those who I love I rebuke and discipline. So be earnest, and repent. Here I am! I stand at the door and knock. If anyone hears my voice and opens the door, I will come in and eat with him, and he with me" (Revelations 3:19–20).

Immeasurably more than we could imagine as the best expression of love from another human being, God loves us even more. Just as we want to communicate and connect with our loved ones, he wants to share in our earthly experience. You and I were created by God, as are all human beings, and he takes great joy in his handiwork. To all who desire to love, just take the time to consider Jesus as he is, research the things in his word that you do not understand, and pray for truth to replace your traditional misconceptions of God. *We must all hold to this one truth: God is love.*

His commandments are there to free us to embrace the gift of life and keep our hearts free from the wreckage caused by our sins on this planet. Seriously, sin separates. Love restores and heals with the gentlest consideration for life. The slogan from my favorite radio station is "God listens," and if we will listen to him, we will learn to do as he does. He loves, heals, and restores. He calls us to step aside from sin and to let his spirit dwell within us so that he and we offer conciliation as we extend, love, healing, and help to restore our fellow human beings in Christ's name. We all share the same calling to minister in right relationships. We cannot minister out of a relationship void of love or without selfless service. Because all self-promoting service is just that, self-promoting, and it has no eternal effect on its recipients. If you give and do well from that empty place of conceit, no one gets a lasting change. *Religion offers short change, and it shortchanges us.*

> Jesus said it, "I am the vine; you are the branches. If a man remains in me and I in him, he will bear much fruit; apart from me you can do nothing" (John 15:5–6).

The vine is in Jesus, and we cannot grow off to the side. We must stay in union with him. The words of Jesus, and the fact that Jesus is the living word, sums up the entire essence of "Immanuel": God with us, and that truth remains eternal. So we can take courage that if we remain on the vine, we will bear fruit. We each must keep our souls open before God and communicate our hearts to him. There is nothing that can be hidden from his sight. In fact, what we think about God is the most important thing about us, and it is the one truth that is self-evident.

Our lives, and the profession of our faith, must grow, until like Christ, we can truly profess a genuinely active and transforming faith, marked by such exemplary love and wisdom, we are freely enabled to understand Jesus' words, "The Father and I are one, and if you have seen anything good in me, it is the work of the Father in me." Do you see the Father of Light and Love at work in your heart, mind, and soul? Are you extending that light and love to help others find the way?

3

Shipwrecked Faith ~ Set Sail Again

*S*t. Paul first coined the term "shipwrecked faith" in his epistle to Timothy.

Timothy, my son, I give you this instruction in keeping with the prophecies once made about you, so that by following them you may fight the good fight, holding on to faith and a good conscience. Some have rejected these and so have shipwrecked their faith (1Timothy 1:18–19).

Many of us have felt the pang of disillusionment when our faith has somehow failed us, and we have given up on God. In times like these, we feel as if our lives are totally wrecked. Just as if you were in a real shipwreck at sea, the possibility that the sinking ship could veritably start to drown us causes panic, which if not responded to wisely could end your life. It is not true if we believe in the moment of our crisis that we are ruined. We can set sail (serve God) again. In the meantime, we can benefit from Paul's analogy if we listen to what he cites as the causes for a shipwrecked faith. Paul warns Timothy that believers who experience faith failure fail to take care of their faith: "Some have rejected these and so have shipwrecked their faith."

When we cease to take care of our faith, the cause is sin, neglect, and error. According to St. Paul's teaching, three primary forces keep our faith on its course. First, we must stay near the Father and exercise our faith and use our spiritual gifts just as Paul instructed Timothy to keep the prophecies given to him. Second, we must fight the good fight, holding onto faith through prayer, worship, and the study of our Bible. Third, we must maintain a pure heart and a clear conscience.

Some have rejected these important aspects of their faith. They stopped drawing near to the Father and exercising their spiritual gifts. They stopped taking the time to pray and study the word of God. They ignored their sin and conscience by harboring grudges that alienated others and broke their connection with God.

The reality is just like the first man, Adam, when our sin becomes public, we feel naked and embarrassed. In our fall from grace, we are beside ourselves—atypical religious wrecks. Weakened by our sin, we turn our backs on our faith and run away to a solitary place to hide, just like Adam hid from God in the Garden. That is the effect of allowing neglect and sin to shipwreck our faith. The good news is God still loves us; he calls our name, and sends the Holy Spirit to restore us with comfort, truth, and counsel. After a faith failure, or shipwrecked testimony, it takes time to repair the damage and rebuild our relationships, but God will heal us according to our need. His plan is a total restoration of our faith and in time, as long as we do not give up our lives, he will make it possible for us to serve (sail) in his name with an even stronger faith.

Many other circumstances may hurt our faith. Perhaps we have lost a loved one to an unspeakable tragedy or a devastating disease. Our hearts are so broken that we mistrust a God who would allow such pain to hurt the unsuspecting. These are the storms of life that throw our ship off its course. We are basically innocent, but our confidence in God is lost. We know that we will heal in time, but we would rather hold onto our pain and continue to tell others how cruel life has been to us. It isn't true. God will lift you up in healing, but you must let him comfort your heart. We may fall, but God still stands. Don't reject his love.

One more reason our faith may shipwreck is that we are not paying attention to the snags under the water. When we find ourselves stuck in a place where we have compromised our testimony, we will not admit our secret shame to anyone, and may get so overwhelmed in humiliation that we abandon our ship of faith and quit trusting in God. Unfortunately, we let pride take over, throw out our failed theology, and replace our faith with a philosophy of life based on our experience. Dealing with a shipwrecked faith is especially devastating when it happens in our youth.

If our shipwrecked faith is a result of the misguided leadership in our churches or denominations, we consider ourselves no better than the masses of people indoctrinated in a pseudo-religious doctrine. Therefore, after having gotten a glimpse that something is wrong with their and our religion, we adopt no religion at all. Worse still, some of us will not honestly listen to our own conscience to see where we deviated from the good fight of faith. We instead give up on the gift of God in our lives and smugly declare ourselves agnostics or deny the existence of God as atheists. *Have you asked honestly, why would we go so far away from our hearts? We don't have to choose to drown ourselves when our faith shipwrecks.* We can get help from God to get safely back to him. His word will guide us to reclaim our faith, find a sounder doctrinal rudder, and serve again with true brethren. The problem is, we are unwilling to forgive others and ourselves when we experience a failure. Forgiveness is a gift. Just ask for it. And when it comes, offer it to others who need it too. *You have to know and trust that God grieves over each one of us when our religious experiences drive us away from our faith and into the empty pursuit of worldly endeavors.*

At this moment, any tender heart hurt by religion from a young age will find comfort as Jesus reminds us how much he values us.

> He called a little child and had him stand among them. And he said: "I tell you the truth, unless you change and become like little children, you will never enter the kingdom of heaven. Therefore, whoever

humbles himself like this child is the greatest in the kingdom of heaven. And whoever welcomes a little child like this in my name welcomes me. But if anyone causes one of these little ones who believe in me to sin, it would be better for him to have a large millstone hung around his neck and to be drowned in the depths of the sea" (Matt 18:2–6).

That sounds harsh, having a stone hung around our neck and drowned in the sea for offending one of God's children, but we must consider that God spoke that warning out of pure love for his creation. Nevertheless, God warns us as older persons of faith: adults, parents, teachers, religious leaders, etc. to be tenderhearted like children (in terms of years on Earth) and converts (in terms of years of conversion). We are not to sin against one another, nor subject one another to rejection or anything else that would uproot or shipwreck our tender, growing faith. Face it. We are in a lot of trouble when we cause someone else's vessel of faith to shipwreck. Let's decide to be humble so as not to hold anyone back from God's love and watch out so our sin is not the root of damage to another person's faith. So much revelation comes to us when we ask the question, "Would God be pleased?"

As it is, we do well to steer clear of condemning others with our conduct or judgments. As his children, our humility and trust in God will guide us to maintain ourselves from giving offense to others. On the other hand, if we do find ourselves offended at no fault of our own, God promises to stand up for us and put down our oppressors. When someone leads another astray, or hurts their belief in God to the point that the child of God loses his faith in the goodness and love of God, then somebody is going to face the truth of their error one day in the presence of God. On that day, knowing there was a better, more beautiful way of living in God's righteousness, is going to demoralize the one who causes another to lose his faith in God. Anyone whose conduct sends people away from the Savior may find that God in turn lets them reap what they have sown.

> But suppose the servant says to himself, "My master is taking a long time in coming," and he then begins to beat the menservants and maidservants and to eat and drink and get drunk. The master of that servant will come on a day when he does not expect him and at an hour he is not aware of. He will cut him to pieces and assign him a place with the unbelievers (Luke 12:45–46).

If you are one who being misguided, misled others into bondage, or embraced a false belief system for a time, you don't need to despair. God is greater than all our weaknesses. His rebuke gives us the knowledge of our sin, and the gift of repentance is ours. Forgiveness is the key through Jesus to all who come to their senses and seek his way. If you feel that you once had faith, but realize it suffered a shipwreck, don't despair. Jesus forgives us for our failures and calls us to live a new way in truth.

> Woe to you experts in the law, because you have taken away the key to knowledge. You yourselves have not entered, and you have hindered those who were entering (Luke 11:52).

> Jesus said, "I am the way, the truth, and the life" (John 14:6).

Even if bad experiences or things that we have done are the cause for our faith to shipwreck, the answer to such disconcerting circumstances still remains that Jesus offers us the way, the truth, and the life. In the upheaval of our faith, when our sin and painful emotions feel unbearable, unforgivable, or as incurable scars on our soul, God's will is forgiveness. We are children of God always, and the invitation to come to him is available now. If we come as he instructs, trusting him like a child, he will draw us to him, heal our child within, and free our hearts to forgive. Let us look at the power of *The Lord's Prayer*.

Jesus said, This, then, is how you should pray: Our Father in heaven, hallowed be your name, your kingdom come, your will be done on Earth as it is in heaven. Give us today our daily bread. Forgive us our debts as we also have forgiven our debtors. And lead us not into temptation, but deliver us from the evil one (Matthew 6:9-13).

The assurance we receive that our sins are forgiven and that the sins of others against us are forgiven is in the words, "Your will be done on Earth as it is in heaven." Since there is no sin in heaven, the forgiveness of all sins, theirs and ours, is his will on Earth. The fact that we should make petition for God's forgiveness daily is the missing power in our belief. The truth the evil one wants to steal from us, so he can keep us stuck in our troubles, is that our forgiveness is secure in Christ. Rejoice as I stress this important thought again! It is God's will that we forgive the sins of others, and he forgives us our sins. One of the reasons Jesus taught us to pray this way is because as his children, any time we are involved in wrongdoing, our faith is in harm's way. If or when our faith falters, we would have nothing without our faith to keep us going on the path of righteousness. Forgiveness keeps our faith alive and healthy. There is not anything as marvelous as walking in forgiveness. Forgiveness opens to us the freedom of connection to share the gift of life with others. Forgiveness is a polish for our character, whose love and joy shines from our hearts and glows in our smiles. *As his jewels, our lives have many facets, and God, through forgiveness, wants to polish them all.*

When we embrace the Lord's will as expressed in his prayer asking him to "Lead us not into temptation, but deliver us from the evil one," the evil one, the prince of this world, has no power to perpetrate our faith or cause it to fail. *The Lord's Prayer* is a perfect example of how we are to align our will to God's will and protect our ministry of service. The way of the Kingdom teaches us that prayer gives us the privilege to be able to honor God as our Father and maintain our relationship with him and others according to his will. We have the responsibility to uphold the standards of our Kingdom (our inheritance) and protect our faith from shipwreck by living truthfully with humility, and loving unconditionally with purity. Prayer makes it possible for us to "fight the good fight of faith"!

To bring things back to our personal situation with faith failure, we unfortunately need to discuss the kind of shipwreck that occurs when we replace our faith with a hypocritical religion. Accepting false teachings, prophecies, or doctrines that are not biblically sound will make you instantly blind to your faith in Christ. Trying to adhere to religious rites of passage or accepting false prophecies to obtain some recognition will appeal to our pride and make us like the Pharisees. To gain recognition and honor among one another, or to earn rewards, these religious people worked to meet the requirements of their own laws and traditions. *By completing the picture as the word made flesh, Jesus fulfilled all the requirements necessary to redeem us from sin and death.* Therefore, we are not to try to honor God like the Pharisees. They kept the laws outwardly and boasted of their knowledge of the law but failed to uphold God's love, mercy, and truth when dealing with others. Consider what Jesus said about himself and the Pharisees in this passage.

> Do not think that I have come to abolish the law or the Prophets; I have not come to abolish them but to fulfill them. I tell you the truth, until heaven and earth disappear, not the smallest letter, not the least stroke of a pen; will by any means disappear from the Law until everything is accomplished. Anyone who breaks one of the least of these commandments and teaches others to do the same will be called least in the kingdom of heaven, but whoever practices and teaches these commands will be great in the kingdom of heaven. For I tell you that unless your righteousness surpasses that of the Pharisees and the teachers of the law, you will certainly not enter the kingdom of heaven (Matthew 5:17).

We need to be careful that our doctrine is not an outward show of our religiosity and that our faith is in Jesus' fulfillment of the law. Our atonement comes from our faith in Jesus, and our salvation in him is the sole basis for our righteousness. Whatever we do, we should do it for God and not for show. There are still false doctrines practiced among modern day Pharisees that tell us we must observe covenants or perform rituals to obtain our salvation and gain eternal rewards. Others tell us to test God's word for worldly gain. Jesus fulfilled the law, and we are complete in him. We need not allow any religious teachings to pronounce judgment on us if we are maintaining our hearts and a clear conscience before God.

Although we live among the deceptions of people who know little of the true nature of God, through Jesus' example we see the way to live in truth and grace. Jesus, God incarnate, reunited us to God, who is our Father. His life is the representation of God's plan to make us one with him in his loving, nurturing, trustworthy, and redemptive nature. The one true faith is all we need to find. If we hold on to our faith with a willingness to obey and learn from the Savior, his example will show us how to share our faith in the right spirit and know if God would be pleased with our religion.

Protecting our faith from wavering is possible as we keep our focus on God. Praying for our daily bread (spiritual wisdom) and honoring God by using his wisdom to keep our conscience clear is a simple solution to keep our troubles from overwhelming our ship of faith. Being genuine before God and others is exactly the kind of wisdom Jesus demonstrated in his humanity. He gave us the blessed model of walking according to the Spirit of God within, and not being pressured by the misguided religious culture. He was obedient to the truth. He responded to life from the love of God, which was the core of his being. *There was never a more genuine person than Jesus, who lived knowing who he was yet remained humble and obedient to God.*

> Your attitude should be the same as that of Christ Jesus: Who, being in very nature God, did not consider equality with God something to be grasped, but made himself nothing, taking the very nature of a servant, being made in human likeness. And being found in appearance as a man, he humbled himself and became obedient to death—even death

on a cross! Therefore God exalted him to the highest place and gave him the name that is above every name, that at the name of Jesus every knee should bow, in heaven and on earth, and every tongue confess that Jesus Christ is Lord, to the glory of God the Father (Philippians 2:5–11).

Had we ever considered it, we would see that Jesus' fully integrated personality, free from sin, enabled him to utilize his full human potential, and this was demonstrated in the compassion he had for others when he performed miracles on their behalf. He knew who he was. He knows who we are. He knows how to love. He loves us as we are. He wants us to know that we are never alone. *Jesus lived with his heart set on pleasing the Father by loving us as we are and helping us find our faith in God. Jesus' love for the Father and the Father's love for Jesus was so complete, they were one in heart, mind, and soul. This is how Jesus' life, fully integrated with God's, became the exact representation of the kind of life God means for all of us to live.* Jesus knew he had what others needed, and he shared it willingly, out of the compassionate love of the Father within. He was the most sincere person who ever lived on Earth. Jesus never had a shipwrecked faith, because he knew in whom and what to believe. "My teaching is not my own." (John 7:16) "It comes from him who sent me." Jesus is the perfect author of our perfect faith.

Jesus lived in communion with his Father, daily accepted his Father's grace, and acted in accordance with his Father's holy plan for life. Jesus demonstrated how our physical and spiritual qualities can work together to accomplish God's work. As long as we are willing to walk in God's will, he will guide us in ways that will keep our faith from shipwreck.

4

Repent ~ Return to the Elementary Principle of Faith

hrough my travels abroad, I once met a Welshmen whose son had died of cancer as a young man. He and his wife had a strong faith and were active in a ministry of charity, but now they refused to attend the church in their village. I asked him why, and he said, "Every mean-spirited person in our village attends the church, so we say our prayers at home." Saddened by his words, I realized I could say the same thing about the climate in a few churches I had attended. Worse than that, I didn't have the heart to tell him that I may have been misguided into seeming like one of those mean-spirited churchgoers. Why and how can you equate churchgoer with mean? It happens when we allow our religion to supersede the expression of our faith. God's anointing is not bestowed upon religion. God anoints his people for service when we repent from preaching church and denomination and return to the elementary principle of Christianity: *Faith!*

On Monday nights, our church had a visitation program for visiting prospects, the sick and the elderly, and any missing active member, provided we had the time. For the most part, we seemed to have a sincere ministry, and maybe we made a difference for some. To this day, I still question what was going on in the minds of our church leaders when they usurped my dedication to visit and reach out to others with a training scheme to send me forth to visit souls as a means to drum up financial support for the church.

Our vision—to reach out and bring the lost to Christ—changed into visiting the homes of our missing church members to reconnect with their tithes. As a dedicated visitor, I had experienced this twice before in other churches, but I apparently missed the science behind it. One year through my role in the yearly church campaign, I received training in canvassing the rosters and going after the missing tithes. Holy Moldy Cheese, something stinks about that! It had a covering of ministry, and there was some touching of hearts and prayer involved, but an underlying motive of the mission was to get a tithe card into the hands of anyone who had ever graced the doors of our church. It wasn't my idea, but I am guilty through involvement.

We followed the program of one of those Church-hired fundraising organizations, which took our money and then told us how to fleece our congregation to get it back. And we accepted this philosophy all because the church body voted to build a brand new extension to our existing and already remodeled sanctuary. Really, do we need the best materials and facilities to serve our Father? Will we only reach out when it benefits our campaigns? Will we continue to make a place for ourselves in this world?

Church has become a business that keeps working to improve its profit margin through its numbers with little thought to its purpose. The foundation of our churches is on the blood of Christ, the Apostles, and the martyrs who laid down their lives for our faith. Wolves were leading the pack of sheep astray, and religious souls like me were following along without even bleating! Ugh! Where did all the shepherds go? Will the true shepherds please wake up, open your eyes, and turn your attention to the call of Christ to care for one another and make disciples, not just tithers? The job of the shepherd is to pastor the flock, not pasture a group of followers, organized neatly around a religious corporation. Have we completely replaced our love for God with our love for our demonization, I mean denomination, so that we no longer care for others? Sorry to shock you with the possibility of that being the source of our resourcefulness, but it is stated in James (3:13-16) that harboring envy and selfish ambition in our hearts is earthly, unspiritual, and of the devil. You tell me, please. Is it the unspoken dream of every head of a church to be able to boast about having the biggest budget, the brightest congregants, and the most modern state-of-the-art churches in the city? Is that the vision people will maintain Sunday after Sunday for eternity?

> For this is what the Sovereign Lord says: "I myself will search for my sheep and look after them. As a shepherd looks after his scattered flock, so will I look after my sheep. I will rescue them from all the places where they were scattered on a day of clouds and darkness" (Ezekiel 34:11–12).

Start looking around you. How many people have entered the desert experience living their profession of faith without a church body caring for them? I am not talking to the lost who have never been saved, converted, christened, churched, or otherwise affiliated with a religious denomination, I am talking about the countless souls, former members of churches, sitting outside the circles of faith, disillusioned, and discouraged. Where are the shepherds who have the heart of Jesus for the flock?

Take the apostles of Jesus, who we can speculate were, for the most part, living outside of the temple. They were probably not involved in regular attendance at the temple because of the highly sophisticated, mean-spirited hypocrites running the House of Worship. The House of Worship had become a social gathering place for the religious who conferred honor and praise on each other. By keeping their outward appearances respectable and ignoring the sin that bound them inwardly, they set themselves up to judge others.

The Pharisees were quick to judge from outward appearance and social standing, and anyone who didn't measure up would feel the sting of their arrogance. They couldn't recognize anyone who came to worship with genuine humility because they didn't have the right attitudes in their own hearts. Their behaviors ostracized many people who left the synagogues and became spiritual outcasts. Sadly enough, today we still have leaders in our churches that have set very strict standards for attendance and tithing. They have concerned themselves with outward shows of religion.

Today, our churches have become pretty standardized in their solicitations and expectations of support. Yes, support of the church is necessary, but let's trust God and stop trusting on the socioeconomic standing of our congregants. Having lost sight of the gospel message, many have become a gathering of the unholy elite who run off the seekers who would be holy if the church was lifting up the teachings of Jesus. The flocks gathered under these Pharisaical shepherds are equally responsible for biting, pushing, and butting heads until the sheep leave and run into the desert. Let us repent and get the word out. Jesus, the Living Word, calls us to worship, not to grow an organization. The spirit of man has been starving to death because the Spirit of God does not come with the bread of communion in every professing body of religious believers.

> If any of you has a sheep and it falls into a pit on the Sabbath, will you not take hold of it and lift it out? How much more valuable is a man than a sheep! Therefore it is lawful to do good on the Sabbath (Matthew 12:11).

> What do you think? If a man owns a hundred sheep, and one of them wanders away, will he not leave the ninety-nine on the hills and go to look for the one that wandered off? And if he finds it, I tell you the truth, he is happier about that one sheep than about all the ninety-nine that did not wander off. In the same way your Father in heaven is not willing that any of these little ones should be lost (Matthew 18:12–14).

> In the temple courts he found men selling cattle, sheep and doves, and others sitting at tables

exchanging money. So he made a whip out of cords, and drove the men from the temple area, both sheep and cattle; he scattered the coins of the money changers and overturned their tables. To those who sold doves, he said, "Get these out of here! How dare you turn my Father's house into a market!" (John 2:15)

This is the most elementary principle in all the faith teachings about our churches. Our Father's house is not a business or a job market for highly paid pastors, ministers, and administrators. It is a place to exercise our faith and worship God. Within our flocks, we must focus our hearts on the elementary principle of faith in Jesus. Like him, we are to keep a watchful and compassionate eye over the sheep scattered all around us. We have a responsibility to love both the lost and the saved, which are not in the fold, and to examine the thoughts and intentions of our hearts.

The so-called spiritual worship, coming forth from the isms, protestants, assemblies, and those who claim to be non-denominational is often carnality offered through perfunctory rituals, or overly emotional, chaotic, and questionable behaviors. For example, let's consider overboard excessive expressions of "worship": loud music, bowing, shouting, corporate recitations, and stomping up and down the aisles, which take our spirit away from God through distractions. We end up listening to or looking at the performers instead of joining them to worship. And who can say if they are truly worshipping either? It can be difficult to pray silently or reach God when our unity is compromised. This is the likes of disorderly gatherings that have little to do with the true and eternal Spirit of God. A good majority of the people attending churches today are taking worship to different extremes. One form is short on self-control, bordering on disorder, and the other is lifeless and mundane, and from the looks of it, the service is on autopilot. Everyone is yawning while its passive congregants are just going through the motions under compulsion of tradition.

Furthermore, some people steeped in religious upbringing seem blinded to how laissez faire their observance of their religion has become. Many who have lived as traditional churchgoers seem incapable of realizing any truth or spirituality outside of their own religious experience. Those feeling confident with their religion deem it must be all right, but dare we trust our feelings?

> Train up a child in the way he should go and when he
> is old, he will not depart from it (Proverbs 22:6).

One could wonder if this scripture binds the souls trained in carnal, self-promoting religion. Many ambitious leaders are preaching prosperity from their pulpits and growing memberships in the thousands. I believe it is time to break up the monopoly of prosperity and get back to the call of Jesus, "Come follow me." God can help us get back to our faith and set aside our established business of creating religious corporations, but it is only going to happen when we repent and look at the difference between the ways we practice our ideas on religion and Jesus' prayerful practice of faith. Jesus' motivation for his body of followers is for us to relate in love. The motivation of some religions seems to be to increase their congregation in numbers and financial providence.

What is the aim of our faith? Sadly, many do not realize that neither the traditional religion nor its modern day counterpart is providing the teaching that Jesus is the bread from heaven. Our sacraments are void of spiritual protein and power, and partaking in them only increases the self-deceptive practices of religion that change no one, at least not for the better. The carnal mind receives it well, as long as we perform our spiritual weekly duty, but the spiritual e coli continue to do damage to the bowels of all involved. Until people totally embrace the truth that God is love, and his love and grace are not for the earning but for the deserving, they will continue to make compulsive, religious attempts to maintain some form of godliness. They will attend church and sacraments, looking to fulfill themselves or enrich their personal comforts while ignoring the necessity of an obedient heart and living a life of faith daily. They will know we are Christians by our Lord. Who is the Lord of our lives?

What you and I really need to do to stop feeling stymied by the entire religious muddle and hasten our spiritual healing is to be alone with God in prayer. Laying aside our misconceptions and becoming transparently honest before God is a positive step toward truth. Taking our time and spending it in prayer will give God an opportunity to renew our minds in spirit and in truth. In a time of prayer, we allow him to chasten us, or bless us as needed for all that is going on inwardly and outwardly with our souls. In this way, we will be preparing our hearts for worship in spirit and in truth. When we approach the Lord in prayer or praise, are we to go before him and express the sins of others? No. We confess our sins and remember that our relationship with our Heavenly Father is about our need for forgiveness and transformation. When we approach God in love, we find the center for our worship is in our hearts, filled with gratitude, and humbled before the Father. True worshipers worship God in Spirit and in truth. That means not even one itsy bitsy lie has a hold on our spirit. True worship means that we are living in the truth, having aligned our spirit to live in obedience to God's will; we cherish life with the utmost respect and adoration for God's goodness and his love for all mankind.

The true imperative is to follow God, trusting his leading as he instructs us daily through the indwelling Holy Spirit, because then and only then will we find the freedom of his grace. His grace is his to offer as he wills. We are recipients and conduits, but we do not have exclusive rights to withhold it from some and offer it only to others. Neither are we able to manipulate favor from the heart of God through religious observances.

> For it is by grace you have been saved, through faith—and this not from yourselves, it is the gift of God—not by works, so that no one can boast (Ephesians 2:5).

Honestly evaluating our thoughts and actions in the light of God's love, and analogically allowing ourselves to undergo a spiritual open-heart surgery through prayer, may be our truest need. This is especially important if we have habitually stopped spending time listening to our inner being. *Time spent with God is time well spent for making us well.* In the book of Acts, the righteous and God-fearing man, Cornelius, had no inclination to know that a Savior had come, yet he lived daily seeking to love God and serve others. Because of the honest and pragmatic purity in Cornelius's heart as he sought after God, in time he received an answer to his prayers through the appearance of an angelic messenger.

I am not saying we can expect God to answer our prayers in such a dramatic way, but the point is, even a nonbeliever has the opportunity to reach God when his heart is pure. Cornelius eventually found the true faith when the Apostle Peter came and brought the gospel of salvation in Jesus. *Apparently, we too may be confident that when we take the initiative to seek God wholeheartedly and not for selfish gain, He places himself closer to our hearts and helps us to take notice of His direct will for us.* Jesus instructed us to pray for the things that we need for our spiritual healing. He tells us that God is a perfect Father who, out of his great love, will provide for us exactly what we need for finding our way to live by faith.

> Ask and it will be given to you; seek and you will find; knock and the door will be opened to you. For everyone who asks receives; he who seeks finds, and to him who knocks, the door will be opened. Which of you, if his son asks for bread, will give him a stone? Or, if he asks for a fish, will give him a snake? If you, then, though you are evil, know how to give good gifts to your children, how much more will your Father in heaven give good gifts to those who ask him! So in everything, do to others what you would have them do to you, for this sums up the Law and the Prophets (Matt 7:7–12).

Knowing this assures us that God will supply our need during our separation in the spiritual desert. We will receive what we need to restore our faith as we ask, seek, and knock with a pure heart. In time, Cornelius's prayers reached God's heart and both Peter and Cornelius were brought together to share the revelation of the gospel of Jesus Christ. There is likewise a restoration for you and me as we diligently seek to have a loving relationship with God. Cornelius and his entire family received salvation through faith and the gift of the Holy Spirit. That is the ultimate spiritual healing, the reconciliation of our lives and our calling through faith in Christ (see Acts 10).

So take heart in your current spiritual state. When we leave behind religious routines that are hindrances to our faith, we will at last have the time to devote to receiving truth from a personal walk with God. Not all the religious ideations preached are evidence of our trust in God. We must beware not to use doctrines to test God's faithfulness to us. In like manner, Satan tempted Jesus to put the Lord's faithful care to the test when he told him to throw himself down from the temple, since it is in the word that God's angels would not let Jesus hurt even one of his feet.

> Then the devil took him to the holy city and had him stand on the highest point of the temple. "If you are the Son of God," he said, "throw yourself down. For it is written: 'He will command his angels concerning you, and they will lift you up in their hand, so that you will not strike your foot against a stone.'
>
> Jesus answered him, "It is also written: 'Do not put the Lord your God to the test.
>
> Again, the devil took him to a very high mountain and showed him all the kingdoms of the world and their splendor. "All this I will give you," he said, "If you will bow down and worship me."
>
> Jesus said, to him, "Away from me, Satan! For it is written: Worship the Lord your God, and serve him only" (Matthew 4:5–10).

Satan also tried to take Jesus' focus off God when he offered him the entire world—if Jesus would just worship Satan. Jesus gave Satan a quick rebuke, and such chastening is likewise for us. We must take warning and examine our religion to see if any of our beliefs or practices is a test to prove God's care for us. God's holiness and mercy still provide the miraculous for believers in answer to prayers of faith. God is mercifully involved in caring for our physical bodies and needs. However, there are many who preach doctrines of healing and prosperity based on our giving to specific ministries in order to receive blessings of healing or financial gain in return. If the goal of our service to God is living in a million-dollar mansion and driving an outrageously expensive car, then maybe we need to redefine exactly which God offered us those things. One wonders how closely we come to testing the Lord as Satan tempted Jesus. Beware of doctrines of worldly blessings that disregard the sufferings of Christ. It's being flaunted around us, but don't be discouraged by these errors.

Take courage that God is raising up many likeminded believers who share in our hunger and thirst for righteousness. By admitting to ourselves that there is a perfect faith and longing for it, even if we temporarily feel agnostic, we are closer to God than the masses of self-deceived Pharisees religiously moving the turnstile in and out of the temple. Keep in mind the row Jesus had with the super religious, and stay encouraged. Although he wept over Jerusalem and loved the Pharisees, he fought with them to restore the one true faith.

Listen to the voice of God, not the shout of religion. Returning to the elementary principles of faith, and regaining a right relationship with our heavenly Father is the subject matter of all Jesus' parables. Jesus' "I AM" statements are more than enough to point us to find faith in him as we consider God telling Moses, "I AM WHO I AM." (Exodus 3:14). "I AM has sent me to you."

> The woman said, "I know that Messiah (called Christ) is coming. When he comes, he will explain everything to us." Then Jesus declared, "I who speak to you am he." (John 4:25-26)

> I am the bread of life. He who comes to me will never go hungry, and he who believes in me will never be thirsty (John 6:35).

I am the living bread that came down from heaven. If anyone eats of this bread, he will live forever (John 6:51).

I am the light of the world. Whoever follows me will never walk in darkness, but will have the light of life (John 8:12).

I am the gate; whoever enters through me will be saved (John 10:9).

I am the good Shepherd. The good shepherd lays down his life for the sheep. The hired hand is not the shepherd who owns the sheep. So when he sees the wolf coming, he abandons the sheep and runs away. Then the wolf attacks the flock and scatters it. The man runs away because he is a hired hand and cares nothing for the sheep. I am the good Shepherd. I know my sheep and my sheep know me. Just as the Father knows me and I know the Father—and I lay down my life for the sheep (John 10:11–15).

Jesus said to her, "I am the resurrection and the life. He who believes in me will live, even though he dies; and he who lives and believes in me will never die" (John 11:25).

I am the way and the truth and the life. No one comes to the Father except through me (John 14:6).

I am the true vine, and my Father is the gardener (John 15:1).

Repentance begins when we are willing to stop and leave behind all our doubtful attitudes and unrighteous actions. The most basic elementary principle is that we must have faith to receive anything from God. Our faith strengthens each time we approach God in prayer and look to his word for our life's needs. His word of truth imparted to us is the foundational rock on which we are to build our faith. To put it simply, we have to stop ignoring the Bible and looking around us for answers. We must study and meditate on God's word, seek guidance through prayer, and listen to God's spirit within.

When we are thirsty for what is right, he is our living water and our righteousness. When we are hungry, he is the bread of life. When we do not know which gate to enter, he is the gate for the sheep. When we are in harm's way, he is the Good Shepherd. When we are fearful of death, he is the resurrection and the life. When we are lost and need direction, he is the way, the life, and the truth. When darkness surrounds us, he is the light of the world. When we want to produce fruit and live a life pleasing to God, he is the vine and we are the branches. Friendship with Jesus is the aim for our life of faith. We only need to tag along with him through the gospels, listen to his parables, and watch the love he extends through his miracles, to see him as he really is. Our greatest need is to be closer to him than anyone or anywhere else on earth. Because he lives, we can become like Able and stop raising Cain in bad behavior.

> Therefore, rid yourselves of all malice and all deceit, hypocrisy, envy, and slander of every kind. Like newborn babies, crave pure spiritual milk, so that by it you may grow up in your salvation, now that you have tasted that the Lord is good (1Peter 2:1).

> We have much to say about this, but it is hard to explain because you are slow to learn. In fact, though by this time you ought to be teachers, you need someone to teach you the elementary truths of God's word all over again. You need milk, not solid food. Not anyone who lives on milk, being still an infant, is acquainted with the teaching about righteousness. But solid food is for the mature, who by constant use have trained themselves to distinguish good from evil (Hebrews 5:14).

Returning to the elementary principle of faith in Christ is not an option if we have embraced a theology that made the focus of our hearts something other than trusting in Jesus. For those of us who want to honor him as Lord, this includes relinquishing our hold on bitterness for offenses; we must ask for and offer forgiveness. Coming to square one is admitting our sin and refusing to harbor the poison of impurity in heart and mind. Our faithful prayer offers us a way to stay close to God, and faith only operates if we turn from self-centered interests and excuses to do wrong, and become genuine seekers for the righteousness that is in Christ. We may have been raised in religion, but now we must first be raised in Christ. It is our gift to receive life from him.

Obeying all the religious rules in the world and attending all its functions will not give us a right relationship with God. Faith in God, in addition to worship in spirit and in truth, is the only way we can keep our connection with God intact. We must faithfully study the life of Jesus and get to know our Lord. With our knowledge and our relationship with Jesus in sync, he will give us the discretion to live as his true disciples. In learning that the Lord is good, we will grow up from needing spiritual guidance to discern how to distinguish between good and evil. A true repentance for falling away from God and seeking His forgiveness for reconciliation is the first principle for living in good faith.

5

Reorganizing Your Religious Reality

For those of us who wish to consider ourselves as followers of Jesus Christ but have been uncertain of how to live by our profession of faith, it might be best to begin by building on a sound, scriptural foundation. The framework of our faith must be based on the Spirit of Truth and aligned with this testimony from the book of 1John.

> Dear friends, do not believe every spirit, but test the spirits to see whether they are from God, because many false prophets have gone out into the world. This is how you can recognize the Spirit of God: Every spirit that acknowledges that Jesus Christ has come in the flesh is from God, but every spirit that does not acknowledge Jesus is not from God. This is the spirit of the antichrist, which you have heard is coming and is already in the world (1John 4:1–3).

Recently, I finished reading and pondering revelations from Prophets of two major denominations. They decided to join hands and support one another because they agreed on the issue of abortion.

However, each holds claim to being the one true church founded by Jesus Christ, and so they look suspiciously on one another's doctrine in respect to their religion. It left me with one nagging question, but what do I know? Are we forsaking the spiritual for the human side of Jesus, or forsaking the human side of Jesus for the spiritual? Moreover, I worry, are we missing Jesus altogether?

It might benefit us, while we are searching, to consider using this philosophical question as a frame of reference. After all, we are in the process of laying a new foundation, remodeling, or reframing our ship of faith. There is one fact that we can be sure to agree on, and that is there is only one true gospel of Jesus Christ. So here follows the question: *How much of your life do you intend to spiritualize when you are part of humanity? If your or my earthly existence was supposed to be lived in a spiritual realm as a spiritual being, then why did Jesus Christ come as a human being and take on flesh and blood? Jesus did not come to reclaim his lost spiritual beings. He came to redeem humanity and heal our spirits.*

Moreover, if you are of those who have a doctrinal spiritual concept of Christ as only a man born of woman, but not as God, then you, as the Bible states in 1John, are embracing the spirit of the antichrist and fall into the category of those who deny that Jesus Christ is both the Son of God and the Son of man. As the Savior of the world, Jesus was God, had all the power and authority of God, but elected to offer truth and mercy to others as the Son of man. He never misused his power to bring glory to himself, but rather, he used it out of love for his brethren. Jesus could bring others to God through his humanity because he was one of us. Jesus did not serve with pride or arrogance. He often instructed others not to publish his gifts of healing because he knew it wasn't about his power, it was about God's mission of redemption.

The antichrist, or as Paul calls him, "the lawless one," will lay claim to being God; he will try to appear to be superior to common humanity, better than human. He will lord over people's hearts and minds, controlling them with powerful deception of his spirituality. His works will appear to be good, but underneath the surface you will find that they are acts of selfishness for his own exaltation and performed without mercy. People will mistake his teachings and miracles to signify his being equal to God. They will not see that what he does for others is only done to gain power and bring others to honor him. Misusing authority, performing the miraculous, and accepting God's glory, as if they are worthy of such adoration, is also the mark of false teachers and prophets.

> Watch out for false prophets. They come to you in sheep's clothing, but inwardly they are ferocious wolves. By their fruit you will recognize them. Do people pick grapes from thorn bushes, or figs from thistles? Likewise every good tree bears good fruit, but a bad tree bears bad fruit (Matthew 7:15–17).

> At that time, if anyone says to you, "Look, here is the Christ!" or, "There he is!" do not believe it. For false Christs and false prophets will appear and perform great signs and miracles to deceive even the elect—if that were possible (Matthew 24:23-24).

> The coming of the lawless one will be in accordance with the work of Satan displayed in all kinds of counterfeit miracles, signs, and wonders, and in every sort of evil that deceives those who are perishing. They perish because they refused to love the truth and so be saved. For this reason, God sends them a powerful delusion so that they will believe the lie and so that all will be condemned who have not believed the truth but have delighted in wickedness (2 Thessalonians 2:9–12).

Jesus didn't come to take anything away from God's creation of humanity or to denigrate being human because Jesus was human. Jesus did not perform miracles to exalt himself, but only to help and heal people as God willed. Jesus is Lord over mankind, but he never lorded over us with spiritual arrogance. Jesus came to take away sin, any one of the seven deadly sins, especially because sin is what degenerates and demoralizes humanity. The antichrist lives by all seven of these detestable sins, but we must not.

> There are six things the Lord hates, seven that are detestable to him: haughty eyes, a lying tongue, hands that shed innocent blood, a heart that devises wicked schemes, feet that are quick to rush into evil, a false witness who pours out lies and a man who stirs up dissension among brothers (Proverbs 6:16).

The problem lies on what we do with the truth of our being both human and spiritual in nature. God created man in his image (Genesis 1:27). When God created man in his image, he breathed the breath of life into him. When we live to either the right or the left of the spiritual and human spectrum, we get out of balance. On one side of our nature, we end up totally spiritualizing our life, walking a spiritual *uptight* rope, always ready to fall into a chasm of despair because we can't stay on the tightrope walk of holiness.

On the other side of our nature, we end up totally humanizing our life, flying on an emotional "trap of ease," swinging back and forth between the spiritual and the carnal, holding to a very humanistic ideation based on our feelings and experiences. *You can become so comfortable with your life you will start excusing anything and everything you do on this planet because, after all, you are only human.* Those attitudes are truly those of a dying breed, whose creed is, "Eat, drink, and be merry because tomorrow you die."

Unfortunately, if that is where our heart is, we had better be aware that we will entirely miss the point of this life. We are here to glorify God and bring the lost to him through our testimony and trust in Jesus. Jesus finished the work for our redemption. So all we need to do is to place our lives into his care, and offer his care to others. Following his call is not an entirely spiritual existence, nor is it an entirely human existence. It is living our existence with the life of faith. Jesus has placed us within his hand to create in us a clean heart and a right spirit. We have his promise that he will keep us safe until he returns us to the Father (see John 10:28–30).

As humans created by God, we have a penchant to tap into the unanswered questions about our eternal purpose. We become frustrated when we must accept that we are not spiritual beings but human beings. We have the capacity to receive a spiritual nature when we are born again of the Holy Spirit through faith in Jesus. The problem lies when we mistake what being born again of the spirit really means for us. If we try to spiritualize ourselves in totality, we will fail to live in our humanity as God has planned. We do become new creatures in Christ when the Holy Spirit comes to dwell within, but we must weigh that with the truth that we have the gift of the Holy Spirit indwelling our earthen, human bodies. Our human birth and life is the experience Jesus shares with us because like us, Jesus had a physical body and came into the world through the birth of a woman. The major difference between Jesus' ability to live a sinless human life and our inability is that Jesus conception was immaculate; our conception contained the sin-spotted seed of Adam. Jesus was spiritually pure yet completely human from birth. We are human from birth and must receive the Holy Spirit to obtain our spiritual inheritance.

> Jesus answered, "I tell you the truth, no one can enter the kingdom of God unless he is born of water and the Spirit. Flesh gives birth to flesh, but the Spirit gives birth to spirit. You should not be surprised at my saying, 'You must be born again'" (John 3:5–7).

Through his humble life as a fellow human being, Jesus lived to show us that our desire to find meaning for our lives can be realized when we acknowledge Jesus as our redeemer and give the Holy Spirit access to our hearts through repentance from self-centered sinning. It is also important for us to note that Jesus was baptized in the Jordan River and also told us to baptize his followers in his name. Some believe that being born of the water is fulfilled through baptism. As Christians, we believe this is a fundamental doctrine from the life and teaching of Jesus. *When we embrace Jesus as our Savior, clear our hearts through confession of sin, and ask for God's will to take priority over our carnal nature and earthly goals, God's Holy Spirit comes to reside in us; it's like we are born again.* When the Holy Spirit comes in, He begins the work of bringing us into a loving relationship with God. Our lives take on meaning and purpose when we cooperate with God's plan to bring all creation back to him through obedience to Christ. In return, Jesus deepens our love.

> If you love me, you will obey what I command. And I will ask the Father, and he will give you another Counselor to be with you forever—the Spirit of truth. The world cannot accept him, because it neither sees him nor knows him. But you know him, for he lives with you and will be in you. Before long the world will not see me anymore, but you will see me. Because I live, you also will live. On that day you will realize that I am in my Father, and you are in me, and I am in you. Whoever has my commands and obeys them, he is the one who loves me. He who loves me will be loved by my Father, and I too will love him and show myself to him (John 14:15–21).

We are not forsaken human beings left without any hope or help to direct our lives on this earth—we have a spiritual dimension hardwired through our intellect and emotions that inspires us. Perhaps our inspiration is the breath of God breathed into our souls on the day of creation. Whatever we may think, we must admit that each of us feels drawn to introspection by our desire to know the truth behind our existence on this planet. We will decide to believe, or not to believe that our lives are a gift designed to have purpose through the plans of an eternal God. We will determine a truth for ourselves to live by.

We cannot deny that we need truth to live. Make no exception, each one will live by a truth—whether it is a spiritual truth, a human truth, a religious truth, or another truth we conclude as our own—it is a foregone conclusion that you are going to live your life by some form of truth. God created you to need an explanation, and like it or not, agnostic, atheistic, or steeped in religious or humanistic convictions, the foundation and framework of your lifestyle finds joy or sorrow in your adopted philosophy. I just want to encourage you to reorganize your religious reality, not begging, borrowing, or stealing your meaning from some pseudo means but seeking to live your life according to the measure of faith and love you have been given.

When questioned by the religious leaders as to which commandment was the greatest commandment in the Law, Jesus' response is the perfect arrangement for anyone who wants to reframe, reorganize, or reform his or her religion.

> Jesus replied: "Love the Lord your God with all your heart and with all your soul and with all your mind. This is the first and greatest commandment. And the second is like it: Love your neighbor as yourself. All the Law and the Prophets hang on these two commandments (Matthew 22:37–39).

Integrate these words into your belief system. Love with your heart, soul, and mind. Embrace them until they resonate with every heartbeat, every thought, and every desire of your being. God wants to indwell you entirely so that your body becomes the temple for his Holy Spirit. Let honesty and integrity be your guide until the life that you are living is a reflection of your pure and loving inner spirit cultivated by faith. Live until God's way, truth, and love is the bedrock for your philosophy of life. Respect the expression of faith through religion, but never allow an empty or false religion to cause you to abandon the teachings of Jesus Christ. Let your faith guide you into the way, the truth, and the life as a child related to God the Father through the Savior Jesus Christ.

It has always been an either/or or neither/nor choice to let the Spirit of truth lead you into the gift of Jesus.

> I am the way, and the truth, and the life. No one comes to the Father except through me. If you really knew me, you would know my Father as well (John 14:6–7).

May we find through prayer a happy and contented rhythm in the thoughts we think, the words we speak, and the actions we take. May we live our lives well knowing that we are always in God's presence when His Spirit lives within us. May we live to the beating of a pure heart, and keep our inner motivation and the timing in our lives ever ready to become a blessing to others and to receive them daily from God for ourselves. Trust me when I tell you that God cherishes all human beings. Every human being is one of his children, and he favors us because we are an individual creation. He treasures the least of them, whosoever they are. His greatest desire is the redemption of his family made in his image. We should appreciate the creator's reflection in every human being and share his heart with them. We are blessed to pray continuously for ourselves and for help in leading others to receive eternal salvation.

Live the questions—ask.
Read the Bible—seek.
Open your hearts—knock.
Enjoy the truth—find.

6

Hope ~ Help for Healing

*B*ack in the seventies, when I first found Christ at a church retreat, I wrote some books of poetry. No, they're not published, but I have them in my keepsake box. I thought it interesting that one line from a poem I'd written all that time ago, after I first accepted Christ, really describes the perspective I've had throughout my lifetime. Here and now, thirty-plus years later, I am going to share this line with you to aid us in our soul searching.

We, each one, must look and consider yesterday, today, and tomorrow—for where, but there, will we find our meaning?

At the time I penned those words, I had no idea how true it rang because I had never read the entire Bible or heard the following scripture:

> Jesus Christ is the same yesterday and today and forever (Hebrews 13:8).

Learning from our past, keeping an eye on our daily business, and looking forward to the future is a wholesome perspective. However, unlike my poem states, our days are numbered, and this lifetime is not the only place to uncover our worth. We should wisely reflect on how we use time, but there is a source of hope that transcends time where we can find what matters most, help for healing our souls. Jesus Christ is the answer for life's meaning that never changes. He is the eternal truth we need to find, and we can find him in our past, present, and future. The truth is, we all need the healing of Jesus more than we need importance. Yesterday, there were people on this planet who needed healing. Today, there are people on this planet who need healing. Tomorrow there will be people on this planet who will need healing. Simple enough, we might consider that yesterday, today, and tomorrow, and throughout our lifetime, our need to heal continues.

Healing is a three-part process that includes rejuvenation of our body, mind, and soul. Through his intelligence and goodness, our Creator provided us with the Trinity for our healing. Some people do not like the word Trinity but forgive the semantics and realize that God revealed himself to us in three persons. We know God as God the Father, God the Son, and God the Holy Spirit. Each person of the divine trinity has brought a different aspect to healing our lives from sin. The missing ingredient in our theology is in understanding that all three persons of the Divine Trinity work in one accord to secure for us our spiritual redemptive healing on Earth and our eternal inheritance in heaven.

The balance of our theology will reveal itself in the way we practice our faith. Faith practices that place an overemphasis on one part of the Godhead to the exclusion of the other two will lose their stability. The complete spiritual healing of salvation designed for the redemption of man was an act of love through the equal contributions of the Father, Son, and the Holy Spirit. The three persons of the Godhead work in unison to redeem us by offering help to heal our bodies, minds, and souls from the pervasiveness of sin and its penalty of death.

God the Father became Immanuel, God incarnate, and through the immaculate conception of Jesus Christ, he created a healing for the human body. By recreating Jesus from the seed of the Holy Spirit, God eliminated the carnal nature and guarded Jesus' human body from sin's effect. Jesus lived a sinless life. Sin brings eternal death, but by indwelling Jesus, God delivered his human body and soul from death in the resurrection. God the Father designed the Immaculate Conception to redeem the physical body from the fall of Adam. This is the Father's part in our redemption. As we consider the prophecies in the Old Testament, they explain the role of God our Creator entering into the human race for the second time to bring salvation to the human body. God the Father worked to heal us from the pronouncement of death that Adam brought to humanity through his sin. Recovery of the human body from the effect of sin is the first area where we needed salvation. Our human body, the one in our genetics, is corrupted by original sin. God's healing of our body in redemption makes it a habitable place for the Holy Spirit. In turn, our salvation provides a place for the Holy Spirit in our lives and assures us of our future resurrection. The physical body is redeemed by the Father.

> Then you, my people, will know that I am the Lord, when I open your graves and bring you up from them. I will put my Spirit in you and you will live, and I will settle you in your own land (Ezekiel 37:13–14).

> I will ransom them from the power of the grave, I will redeem them from death. Where, O death, are your plagues? Where, O grave is your destruction? (Hosea 13:14).

> Therefore, the Lord himself will give you a sign: the virgin will be with child and will give birth to a son, and will call him Immanuel (Isaiah 7:14).

> For unto us a child is born, to us a son is given, and the government will be on his shoulders. And he will be called wonderful Counselor, Mighty God, Everlasting Father, and Prince of Peace (Isaiah 9:6).

Jesus' role in the plan of redemption is to bring healing to our patterns of thinking. God the Son became the Word made Flesh, redeeming our minds. Jesus opened our minds to think spiritually with parables.

> The Word became flesh and made his dwelling among us. We have seen his glory, the glory of the One and Only, who came from the Father, full of grace and truth (John 1:14).

We think in a transformed way when Christ renews our mind with the gospel. By bringing to us the light of the truth, Jesus removed sin and our bondage to darkness with its evil thoughts, condemnation, and guilt. He restores our thoughts to view life from God's loving perspective. Jesus, the living word, through the teaching of the word, restored our ability to be converted into the children of God. Through his grace, we embrace healing to receive a new mind, the mind of Christ. Consider the scriptures in reference to Jesus. It is the work of the Son of God to illuminate our mind's eye. Jesus heals our intuition so that through our believing, we are able to comprehend the miracle of our salvation and live born again as the children of God. Jesus gave our minds a complete paradigm shift. The physical mind is redeemed by the Son of God.

> The true light that gives light to every man was coming into the world. He was in the world, and though the world was made through him, the world did not recognize him. He came to that which was his own, but his own did not receive him. Yet to all who received him, to those who believed in his name, he gave the right to become children of God—children, born not of natural descent, nor of human decision or a husband's will, but born of God. The word became flesh and made his dwelling among us. We have seen his glory, the glory of the One and Only, who came from the Father, full of grace and truth (John 1:9–14).

The Holy Spirit's role in the plan of redemption is to bring healing to our will. Our will is our source of inner wisdom. Our freedom to make choices is within our will, which is at times referred to as our heart or soul. There is much interpretation in the Bible regarding the words heart, soul, and spirit, but interchangeably they mean the inner man. Using our free will gives us the ability to choose between God's goodness or Satan's evil. God the Holy Spirit redeems our will with truth so that we could receive the healing necessary to restore our broken fellowship with God. God the Holy Spirit became our Counselor bringing peace to our hearts and to help us avoid the trouble of wrong choices. Most importantly, the Spirit of Truth brought conviction of sin to the world, opening the way for us to decide for our repentance, leading us back to God, and restoring our free will from the contamination of unrighteousness. The spirit, soul, and will of man are redeemed by the Holy Spirit.

> All this I have spoken while still with you. But the Counselor, the Holy Spirit, whom the Father will send in my name, will teach you all things and will remind you of everything I have said to you. Peace I leave with you; my peace I give you. I do not give to you as the world gives. Do not let your hearts be troubled and do not be afraid (John 14:25–27).

> But I tell you the truth: it is for your good that I am going away. Unless I go away, the Counselor will not come to you; but if I go I will send him to you. When he comes, he will convict the world of guilt in regard to sin, because men do not believe in me; in regard to righteousness, because I am going to the Father, where you can see me no longer; and in regard to judgment, because the prince of this world now stands condemned. I have much more to say to you, more than you can now bear. But when he, the Spirit of truth, comes, he will guide you into all truth (John 16:7–13).

Until we accept God's will for our salvation, we are continually bearing the condemnation of a guilty conscience for our sin, the result of breaking spiritual laws. In addition, we may unknowingly or knowingly burden others who reap the consequences for our wrongdoing. Humanity, weakened by sin after the fall of Adam and Eve, has been unable to share in God's holiness. Sin, if not atoned for, brings perpetual death and severance from a holy God. Through Abraham and Moses, God gave us laws and initiated sacrifices to teach us that sin has a penalty of death. Now it is the work of the Holy Spirit to show us how to renounce sin. At the time of Jesus' ministry on Earth, religious leaders had traded the ministry of faith for adherence to hundreds of prescribed rules they added to the laws of Moses. Jesus ended the need to atone for sin through sacrifice, and he fulfilled the law. In faithful obedience to God, he became the sacrifice for our sins. Coming to Christ in repentance secures God's forgiveness for our sins and lawless acts. When Jesus and the Holy Spirit are invited into our lives, God puts his laws into our hearts and writes them on our minds.

> This is the covenant I will make with them after that time, says the Lord. I will put my laws in their hearts, and I will write them on their minds. Their sins and lawless acts I will remember no more. And where these have been forgiven, there is no longer any sacrifice for sin (Hebrews 10:16–18).

God knew the weakness of man and our inability to keep our lives free from sin through the observance of the law alone. God sent the Holy Spirit to create in us a new life of faith. The Holy Spirit within restores our freedom of will to love God with all our strength, heart, mind, and soul. The first miraculous act of the Holy Spirit indwelling a human was Mary's conception of Jesus. God became incarnate and sent us the Word, Jesus Christ in the flesh. It is the Holy Spirit who puts the laws of God into our hearts so we will want to please him. It is Jesus the Word who puts the laws of God into our minds so that our thoughts will please him. It is God the Father who put himself into humanity as God incarnate through his only begotten Son. It is God who redeems our body and honors us by allowing our body to become a temple of the Holy Spirit.

Adam was created in God's image but fell through sin. Jesus, who is sometimes called the second Adam, is a human being with a human mother, but he is free from the sinful nature passed on to all other human beings. At his conception, the Holy Spirit began living within his body giving him the power of will to overcome the sin nature in Mary's genes. Jesus is the first human being to remain holy and to overcome sin with the spiritual willpower of our Heavenly Father. Jesus' inner motivation in life was his desire to fulfill the will of God in becoming our Savior. Jesus lived daily in communion with God by choosing to listen to and follow the voice of God's indwelling Holy Spirit. Jesus demonstrated God's love to all as he brought grace and truth to us. Through Jesus, we too have been reconciled to relate to God as our Father.

> From the fullness of his grace we have all received one blessing after another. For the law was given through Moses; grace and truth came through Jesus Christ. No one has ever seen God, but God, the One and Only, who is at the Father's side, has made him known (John 1:9–16, 17).

These foundational truths of the gospel are good news for us. The word states that we receive blessing after blessing once we are born again of the same Holy Spirit. We can do the work of God and exemplify the fruits of the Holy Spirit in our daily lives just as Jesus did. Without the Holy Spirit, we would remain unredeemed human beings with the gene pool of Adam and an unrequited carnal nature. Alone without a relationship with God, we are helpless to stop the flow of our bent to sin. The gospel tells us that if we seek after the Lord for our salvation, we will receive redemption. Salvation is available to all who call on the Lord with a sincere heart of faith. Redemption after salvation is the work of the Holy Spirit who draws us to Jesus, who draws us to the Father. And the Holy Trinity provides a complete inner healing.

> But the fruit of the Spirit is love, joy, peace, patience, kindness, goodness, faithfulness, gentleness, and

> self-control. Against such there is no law. Those
> who belong to Christ Jesus have crucified the sinful
> nature with its passions and desires. Since we live
> by the Spirit, let us keep in step with the Spirit
> (Galatians 5:22–25).

After spending the past ten years of my yesterdays feeling caught in a never-ending undertow, spinning from one sorrow of life into others, including breast cancer, multiple surgeries, eight rounds of chemotherapy, and a long time away from the weekly practice of corporate worship, I am finally and painfully aware of this one truth. It doesn't matter where you're coming from, or where you've been. One thing I know is that you can't blame God when your faith fails. The fact is, your faith will be dead to you if you are dead to your faith.

> St. Paul: No temptation has seized you except what
> is common to man. And God is faithful; he will not
> let you be tempted beyond what you can bear. But
> when you are tempted, he will also provide a way
> out so that you can stand up under it (1Corinthians
> 10:13).

What is it that we forget when our sorrows take us into the desert? *God is faithful!* We are the ones who fail. It's time to take a look at our fruits. It may very well have been a lot of the proverbial them (other people) or the tragedies of life (sin, disease, and death) causing our problem yesterday, and if we could, we would definitely avoid the problematic in our walk of faith. HOWEVER, what is it that you or I know about our personal faith, or lack of faith that needs renewal today? It's not about the religious leaders or other believers who let us down. We cannot blame anyone if we refuse the grace of God. We don't have the right kind of wisdom if we think we are wise enough to point the blame on someone else for the way we respond. It is not our place to judge the sins of our brothers and sisters, the lost, or the hypocrites. You and I have to keep our eyes on Jesus and let him help us clean up our inner souls. We do God's will when we pray for, rather than prey on, one another.

If you or I want to come home tomorrow or in the near future, we have to know where our home is. *If we want to have a healthy, living faith, today and tomorrow, we need to place our trust and hope in our heavenly calling. God comes to us in the fullness of the Godhead.* God is holy, and if we are going to call on God, we have to be as perfect as our perfect Father in heaven. What I am saying is, we can't hold on to our sin with one hand and reach for God with the other. Sin will dirty both hands, and God will have no part of sin. If we do not repent and pray, we will lose another day grasping for something Jesus' healing has already provided. He is everything we need!

Breathe in and out and imagine how it feels to have the warmth and light of the morning sun gently shining upon us. Look out the window and see its shadows cast upon the ground. Its light falls upon the earth everyday and its heat intensifies at each passing hour. We feel grateful when we embrace this gift of light with its unique kindness. We find rest in the special warmth that only the sunshine can give. We relish its healing and calming qualities. The privilege is that whenever we choose, we can take one perfect moment to bask in the miracle of this light and experience the joy of this part of our world. Some ancient people so inspired by this celestial body of light have declared that the Sun is a god. The based-on-fact reality is that the sun is a star, not a god. Its light and warmth provides health for the earth, but its work of shining on our planet has only a physical effect.

Truth is we need something more than a physical light to live by. Having warmth from the sunshine on our shoulders is not enough to keep our hearts and minds pure. In a similar way, just as our physical bodies find respite in the physical sun, our spiritual nature needs a spiritually pure and wholesome healing light to live and walk by daily. Just as we are physically awed to inspiration by the gentle embrace of the morning sun, we can be spiritually awed to inspiration by the gentle embrace of the Son of God.

> In the beginning was the Word, and the Word was
> God. He was with God in the beginning. Through

> him all things were made; without him nothing
> was made that has been made. In him was life, and
> that life was the light of men. The light shines in
> the darkness, but the darkness has not understood
> it. (John 1:1–5)

Could we understand if we had God's healing light omnipresent within us? What if the darkness inside us could be brought to the light? What if the light of God replaced the darkness of the sin nature that dwells inside of us? Couldn't we feel grateful if we were cleansed and given a clean spiritual feeling of rest, warmth, and peace in our every living moment? Breathe in and out and imagine how it could feel to have the eternal love of God's healing light omnipresent inside you. And prayerfully read the words to follow because they're accurate:

> This is the message we have heard from him and
> declare to you: God is light; in him there is no
> darkness at all. If we claim to have fellowship with
> him yet walk in the darkness, we lie and do not live
> by the truth. But if we walk in the light, as he is in
> the light, we have fellowship with one another, and
> the blood of Jesus, his son, purifies us from all sin
> (1John 1: 5–7).

There is an actuality expressed in this scripture, the certainty of us living in the purity of God's spirit of light, just as surely as we walk daily in the reality of the sunlight by day and the moon and the stars by night. "God is light; in him there is no darkness at all." God provides a spiritual light for our lives, a light to heal us from impurity and sin. When we allow his spirit to shine on our lives, we experience a therapeutic restoration within our souls. His chaste and wholesome light surrounds us and connects us to live in unity and fellowship with others. How many years have we been on the outside refusing to look inside our soul? We can stop living in the stage of blaming others ... or even in blaming ourselves for our faith failures and past regrets. Today, we can address the longing in our hearts, minds, and souls to live a life full of light, warmth, and love, as we look to the original resource. God is not only love, God is light.

> This is the message we have heard from him and declare to you: God is light; in him there is no darkness at all (1John 1:5).

> When Jesus spoke again to the people, he said, "I am the light of the world. Whoever follows me will never walk in darkness, but will have the light of life" (John 8:12).

Jesus is the provision of God for us. He is a miraculous, healing light. He is the word made flesh. When we repent from our prideful, self-seeking attitudes and allow His spirit to come in, He will cleanse our hearts from sin and make his home within. The "aha!" moment of rest can be with you every minute of your day as you walk humbly in obedience to what the Spirit of God is responsible for in your life. Our health, happiness, and hope for the heavenly existence, his will to be done on Earth as it is in heaven, depends on our coming home to legitimacy, becoming Children of God, and taking a position to live faithfully beside him.

It is simply about you and God. It's only about me and God. You and I must, on our own, sit calmly before him in spirit and truth. We need to worship God with a humble attitude and truthful communication through prayer with his Spirit. Each person must do this for himself daily. Today is the day given us to start letting God untangle the web of sorrow, those past involvements, years of lies, neglect, and sin. If we will bring it to him and admit our desire to live in his light, his aspiration and will is to cleanse our souls of anything of darkness that causes regret and to replace it with the light that causes healing.

We, each one, must look and consider our lives in Jesus Christ yesterday, today, and tomorrow—for where, but there, will we find spiritual healing?

Consider the scriptures and remember what you learned about God yesterday. Hold on to what you know about God today. Have hope in what God says about tomorrow.

> For God so loved the world that he gave his one and only Son that whoever believes in him shall not perish but have eternal life (John 3:16).
>
> For God did not send his Son into the world to condemn the world, but to save the world through him (John 3:17).
>
> Whoever believes in him is not condemned, but whoever does not believe stands condemned already because he has not believed in the name of God's one and only Son (John 3:18).
>
> This is the verdict. Light has come into the world, but men loved darkness instead of light because their deeds were evil. Everyone who does evil hates the light, and will not come into the light for fear that his deeds will be exposed. But whoever lives by the truth comes into the light, so that it may be seen plainly that what he has done has been done through God (John 3:19–21).

In the meantime, for yesterday, today, and tomorrow, let's accept the exhortation to grow in faithfulness, to daily remain tenderhearted, and to not lose our way to fulfill our calling to God. And let us take the warning from the scripture not to be those who fall away and produce thorns and thistles. Let's drink in the rain of God's grace and uphold his word. And let's not turn our backs on the heavenly gift of the Holy Spirit and subject our Savior and our Christianity to public shame.

> Therefore let us leave the elementary teachings about Christ and go on to maturity, not laying again the foundation of repentance from acts that lead to death, and of faith in God, instruction about baptisms, the laying on of hands, the resurrection of the dead, and eternal judgment. And God permitting, we will do so. It is impossible for those who have once been enlightened, who have tasted

the heavenly gift, who have shared in the Holy
Spirit, who have tasted the goodness of the word
of God and the powers of the coming age, if they
fall away, to be brought back to repentance, because
to their loss they are crucifying the Son of God all
over again and subjecting him to public disgrace.
Land that drinks in the rain often falling on it and
that produces a crop useful to those for whom it is
farmed receives the blessing of God. But land that
produces thorns and thistles is worthless and is in
danger of being cursed. In the end it will be burned
(Hebrews 6:1-8).

For many of us, our past behaviors and thought life was impure
and misdirected in personal sin, a nominal life of religion, a dead
practice of disregarding the gift of our salvation, and refusing to allow
the Holy Spirit to complete our redemption. If we have embraced
Christ as our Lord, we must not go backward to our old patterns of
self-centered thinking. Instead, we can choose to take the faith of
Jesus, pray with him to our heavenly Father, and look forward with
anticipation that God the Holy Spirit will make his home in our
hearts. Daily prayer is our daily bread.

Prayer is an act of hope, the key to our restoration. Hope draws
us to seek. Seeking leads us to faith. Faith leads us to ask God to
abide in our hearts. God honors our faith with the gift of the Holy
Spirit. The Holy Spirit comes to live in us and gives us a fresh
spiritual beginning. His life welling up from inside us is like a spring
of living water, washing over us and refreshing us with the cleansing
stream of forgiveness. God's omnipresent endless love provides our
spiritual peace with light flowing down from heaven and entering
our earthly bodies. We have the privilege of being called the children
of God. With that comes the responsibility for choosing to live daily
in the light and truth of his grace.

Today, as we keep our concentration fixed on God's warning
and his promises, words like these from St. Paul the Apostle will
safeguard us from wandering off again into the desert away from

our faith. God will heal us and help us obtain the truth we sincerely desire in order to live closer to Christ.

> So as the Holy Spirit says: "Today, if you hear his voice, do not harden your hearts as you did in the rebellion, during the time of testing in the desert, where your fathers tested and tried me and for forty years saw what I did. That is why I was angry with that generation, and I said, 'Their hearts are always going astray and they have not known my ways.' So I declared on oath in my anger; 'They shall never enter my rest.'"
>
> See to it, brothers, that none of you has a sinful, unbelieving heart that turns away from the living God. But encourage one another daily, as long as it is called, today, so that none of you may be hardened by sin's deceitfulness. We have come to share in Christ if we hold firmly till the end the confidence we had at first. (Hebrews 3: 7–15)

Hear and believe God's voice within you. Feel and see how his light shines upon you. Accept how his spirit gently extends hope to heal you. Take all he offers and find needed rest for your body, mind, and soul. God knows where we are and why we are there. Why do we live as if he does not know or care? When we seek him with all of our heart, we will find him, and when we do, he promises to bring us out of the captivity of our spiritual dryness, out of the desert, and into his hopeful plans for our future. God himself (in three persons) is our hope and help for a complete (three-dimensional) healing.

Whatever has caused our separation, God does not forget us. God forgives us. We are called to be honest. We are blessed to follow him in works of righteousness.

Our Creator was there in our yesterdays, He is here in our today, and He will be there in our tomorrow. God is faithful to help us find Jesus nearby in yesterday, today, and tomorrow. God's insurance policy includes plans for healing our lives from the futility of our darkened understanding. He desires to heal us from sin, and his promise that if we will seek Him, we will find Him is the same promise given yesterday, today, and tomorrow.

> For I know the plans I have for you, declares the Lord, plans to prosper you and not to harm you, plans to give you hope and a future. Then you will call upon me and come and pray to me, and I will listen to you. You will seek me and find me when you seek me with all your heart. I will be found by you, declares the Lord, and will bring you back from captivity (Jeremiah 29:11–14).

7

Forsaking Futility or Falling Away ~ Finding Faith in the Desert

*T*here was a great revival in the desert when a man in camel skin clothing began to preach that the Kingdom of heaven was near. Droves of people left the Pharisees behind in the synagogue and went to this forsaken piece of land because their hearts were hungry for God. Starving on a diet of religious traditions and manmade laws, meted out with the judgment of the Pharisees and the teachers of the law, the message of repentance and baptism must have been very refreshing. The word spread in all the area around Judea that God wanted a relationship with his people's hearts and all they needed to do was repent from sin. No Pharisaical requirement was necessary. The burden of trying to make one acceptable to God through obeying the rules and performing rituals was no longer in effect. John the Baptist was preaching repentance from sin to those who had fallen away and offering freedom to those who wanted to forsake the futility of religion. In addition, many sinners and tax collectors rejected by the Pharisees, and other outcasts from the synagogue repented and were baptized. Among those baptized by John were the disciples Andrew,

John, and Peter. God was introducing a new way to make atonement for sin. Through this revival people's hearts were being made ready to receive Jesus as the Lamb of God. Jesus' death on the cross is in fulfillment of God's promises for a Messiah.

Interestingly, the first message for repentance and baptism recorded in the New Testament came from John the Baptist. At that time, it was a significant place for having faith in God restored. The people flocking to hear John the Baptist's preaching to repent from sin were hearing of a way to relate to God without having to be oppressed and burdened by the religious system taking place in the synagogue. The point is God works in our hearts and that doesn't require a building. Jesus did not appoint the twelve to follow him at a church committee meeting. Instead, Jesus found them as they were going along living their daily lives. They didn't miss out on Jesus because they weren't in church. The truth they heard in the desert listening to John the Baptist made their hearts hunger for righteousness. For some of us, God allows us to have this time of separation from church so that He may instruct us in grace and truth. In the heart of every man is the just desire for love and truth, and that's what drew people to John the Baptist and eventually to Jesus.

> I will send my messenger ahead of you, who will prepare your way, a voice of one calling in the desert, "Prepare the way for the Lord, make straight paths for him."

> And so John came, baptizing in the desert region and preaching a baptism of repentance for the forgiveness of sins. The whole Judean countryside and all the people of Jerusalem went out to him. Confessing their sins, they were baptized by him in the Jordan River (Mark 1:2–5).

John wasn't preaching about what they needed to do to uphold the traditions or the laws of the Pharisees. John was preaching the doctrines of repentance and baptism for the forgiveness of sins. He was telling everyone that God was offering them forgiveness for the sin that was wrecking their lives. What do you think? When the sinners went to the desert to hear John, were they forsaking the futility of their religion, or falling away from it? Were they just interested in seeing John perform baptisms? Or do you think many went out to hear John because they were trying to find the truth for what it means to have faith in God? John opened the way for faith.

> After John's messengers left, Jesus began to speak to the crowd about John: "What did you go out into the desert to see? A reed swayed by the wind? If not, what did you go out to see? A man dressed in fine clothes? No, those who wear expensive clothes and indulge in luxury are in palaces. But what did you go out to see? A prophet? Yes, I tell you, and more than a prophet. This is the one about whom it is written: I will send my messenger ahead of you who will prepare your way before you" (Luke 7:24–27).

> All the people, even the tax collectors, when they heard Jesus' words, acknowledged that God's way was right, because they had been baptized by John. But the Pharisees and experts in the law rejected God's purpose for themselves, because they had not been baptized by John (Luke 7:29–30).

If we have been avoiding the confines of corporate weekly worship services for any length of time, most people will think we have fallen away from God. That is not necessarily so. Some who are disconcerted with their churches stop their attendance to forsake the futility of empty practices of religion. Others may be out of church because a series of heart breaking storms wrecked what little faith they had. To be merciful to the believers, most of us don't just quit one day and walk out on our faith. We don't make a conscious effort to head to the desert, we usually head to the desert because life has thrown us some curves and we need time to get it straightened out. Maybe going to a barren place makes room for the fullness of God!

Trials can push us out of our religious comfort zone and take us into spiritual desolation in our attempt to get away from it all. Things like rebellion in our children, depression, marital discord, cancer, loss of our parents or children, the death of close friends, and confrontations with false teachers, doctrines, and Pharisees are enough to make us fighting mad. And when we get angry, we want to blame our problems on our family, friends, church, and God. We may get so offended, we offend others who direct us to the door and slam it in our faces, or maybe we leave and slam the door behind us. The point is anger, hurt, and heartache will drive you into lonely places. When it all settles, we may find ourselves more confused than ever. We may not be able to get the story straight. That's how many of us end up in pain trying to reclaim our faith in the desert.

If we nurse our anger in the desert, we can go numb. We may refuse to acknowledge the pangs of loneliness we feel when we are out of sync with God and our fellows. Anyone who has been disconnected from their fellowship after having been active in their church body may feel that they are experiencing phantom limb pain. When there are no letters, calls, concern, or visits, we may constantly ache for the missing body. We long for anyone who genuinely cares in Christ's name, and sometimes nobody comes. The church as a whole continues its functions and doesn't seem to notice the people they've abandoned or their sorrow. When you have been a contributing and faithful church member for a long time, it is possible to develop a root of bitterness toward your former associates who have moved on without you. The sad part is how long we may stumble around in our condition of disillusionment, not realizing that we are, in fact, in spiritual crisis. Needless to say, it may take years of wandering in this state of spiritual confusion before we know that we are not going to come out without God's healing. Until we start seeking God, we may not be able to clearly see our past or understand what we need to do to get out of the lonely desert.

If we are out of our religious practice because of burn out from church service, we may feel remorse for having used our faith as a tool for religious or prideful purposes. In the heart of every true believer is the assurance that God has given us salvation, the Holy

Spirit, and spiritual gifts that we are to exercise through our faith. Unfortunately, many energetic Christians become overloaded with religious obligations. We take on the responsibilities gladly, but over time we find our faith suffocating under the dead works we are performing to please our church and ourselves. When exhaustion sets in after spiritual burnout, we have nowhere to go except to a solitary place for rest.

Another form of burnout happens when we run to and from church meetings, conferences, events, revivals, and Bible studies involving all our time in an endless stream of activities for years. We may accumulate so much mental knowledge that we end up with a bad case of religiosity. Some people are so sickeningly religious it makes them and everyone else around them ill. No kidding! Some people are addicted to religion, and maybe you know one of them. When religion and church become our opium, the only recourse is to get out of the church so you can get the church out of your system. This too is the result of futility.

Remember Saul, so full of his religion, a Pharisee of Pharisees, zealously traveling for the church persecuting the Christians? Yet he somehow missed God. A zillion praises to our merciful God because he knows us better than we know ourselves. Sometimes, with his full knowledge and great wisdom, he cuts us off at the pass, allows us to be chastened, and sets us aside alone in the spiritual desert for a season. This is what he did for the Apostle Paul. After Paul was well on his way to hurting every believer in his path including himself, he was kindly blinded by Jesus on the road to Damascus. Jesus rebuked him for persecuting the Lord. Helpless and blind, he was led to the house of Judas on Straight Street. Ananias was given a vision of Paul. Paul was given a vision of Ananias. Ananias came and placed his hands on Saul for healing, and then Paul could see again. God revealed to Ananias that Paul would be his messenger to take the gospel to the Gentile world (see Acts 9:1–19).

Paul spent all his life living in the power of his religious credentials, and he was active in the persecution of Christians. After his salvation, he went into the desert to spend time alone seeking God and getting his life straightened out. With both a born-again salvation experience and the former persecution of Christians on his résumé, there weren't many Paul could trust in fellowship, or who would trust him. This may be in part why he separated himself and spent three years in the desert before introducing himself to Peter and the believers in Jerusalem. After this, Paul did not go back to the church in Judea for another fourteen years. That's seventeen years of growing in the Lord and serving him outside the original body of Jesus' followers.

> But when God, who set me apart from birth and called me by his grace, was pleased to reveal his Son in me so that I might preach him among the Gentiles, I did not consult any man, nor did I go up to Jerusalem to see those who were apostles before I was, but I went immediately into Arabia and later returned to Damascus. Then after three years, I went up to Jerusalem to get acquainted with Peter and stayed with him fifteen days. I saw none of the other apostles—only James the Lord's brother. I assure you before God that what I am writing you is no lie. Later I went to Syria and Cilicia. I was personally unknown to the churches of Judea that are in Christ. They only heard the report: "The man who formerly persecuted us is now preaching the faith he once tried to destroy." And they praised God because of me.
>
> Fourteen years later, I went up to Jerusalem, this time with Barnabas. I took Titus along also. I went in response to a revelation and set before them the gospel that I preach among the Gentiles (Galatians 1:15–2:2).

I shared that so you could understand that whether you are disheartened and forsaking the futility of religion, or are disillusioned and have fallen away from the Lord because of the storms of life, you can find your faith. People continuously want to beat us up when we are not looking like their idea of a church crusader Christian, but God is working on our hearts. Staying true to him will sometimes mean that we are going to stay out of church. Don't let anyone make you think that you are or will always be antichurch, antireligious, or hopeless as a believer. Everyone should realize that God always has better plans for us than anyone, even better than the plans we have for ourselves.

It is possible and highly probable that God lets us wander around in this solitude a while because he is trying to do a work in us, between him and us alone, without the interference of our former religious ideology or associates. Our time of separation is a time to decide for God, to learn to obey his voice, and to allow him to make changes in our character. Seeking God with all our heart will lead us to find his best in an honest walk of faith.

We'll know that we are growing in honesty and goodness when we no longer desire to see through denominational eyes, be motivated self-righteously, think critical thoughts, speak unwholesome words, or act like demonized bigots. We will know that we are softening into a gentle spirit when we refuse to point the finger of judgment at anyone else. We may find our faith returning to us with a renewed attitude of love for our neighbors. As we humbly yield to God's Holy Spirit, we will reach out in compassion to offer God's healing touch to others. If our healing has been drying out from the intoxication of our pseudo spirituality, we'll know we have become sober when we learn that God resists the proud but gives grace to the humble. After years of solitary refinement in isolation, our consolation is a humble, forgiving faith.

If your story or the story of someone you know went something like this, perhaps you will relate. Some time ago, there was a faithful church member who proudly went to lead and teach in many weekly meetings. This person was clueless that he was living a religious life of futility and often wore a futile expression on his face. From outward appearances this was a good religious person, all dressed in his Sunday best. He had no clue that his temple housed an impure box full of bad and ungrateful attitudes. It galled him that no one seemed to appreciate his efforts to manage the church.

We'd watch him get so upset, acting double minded, and stumbling around, blinded by his frustration with everyone around him. He just couldn't see that things were not going well for him under the surface, but others saw right through to the dark pain inside. He needed a face-to-face with the facts going on inside his soul. He was sowing his life together with the discontented seeds of religion, but because he did not sew up a loving relationship with Jesus, his life came unraveled at the seams. Finally, to all outside observers, he appeared to be just another lost hypocrite. Actually, maybe he wasn't. Maybe he was sincerely trying to find God through his religious endeavors but didn't have a clue about the freedom of walking by faith. Perhaps God was allowing him all those years to get to the end of his religion, so he could hunger for a relationship with God. Be careful not to judge when you see a soul stuck in a works rut, because God may be letting them work their way into the desert where the Holy Spirit will be waiting to reunite with them in faith.

All that hurt and emptiness could be what has happened to some of us. But finding faith in the desert will take away all the fear, all the failures, and all those seemingly wasted years will make us over comers. The emotional distress caused by sorrow, our sin, the sifting of the devil, the people who persecuted us, the false religious doctrines, and uncharitable acts of others doesn't have to control us or our memories anymore. God does his great work of healing our spirit through repentance. When we turn from sin, and turn to him, he blankets our emotions in the warmth and security of his love and forgiveness.

God helps us find our faith as he keeps extending forgiveness to us. Forgiveness brings healing to our souls. When we finally grasp the idea that Jesus offers forgiveness to the whole world, and believe in living according to the Holy Spirit, we will be healed. On the other hand, if we refuse his love and hold onto sinful, unforgiving attitudes and run over others with criticism and misjudgment, we will stay under sin's control.

Sin is a nasty and horrible overlord. If we are controlled by the enemy, day after day, he will lord over our spirit with condemnation and regrets. He is overbearing and tears down our faith. Repentance is the only thing that stops sin's beast. When we are willing to embrace Jesus, accept his forgiveness, and cry out for deliverance from our sins, this puts the overlord on notice.

Jesus comes to our defense when he hears our prayers. Through the forgiveness we receive and offer others, the dragon breathing the fire of hell into our thinking will be spayed. (LOL! I said spayed so he cannot continue to reproduce lies.) Our call to Jesus for deliverance becomes our victory.

An Overstatement

We cannot overstress our overwhelming need to find an overmatch, to overpower, and overmaster, the Overlord, who's overmuch overrunning has become an overload that we cannot overlook overnight. So would you please oversee, overrule, override, and overturn the overweening, overbearing Overlord who has overstepped and overstayed to the point that we are overwrought, and overwriting, an overflowing, overdue desire to be over joyous in presenting to the Overlord's overhearing our final overture:

It is Over!

Thanks to God in Christ Jesus! The frustration of sorting through the labyrinth of sin in our minds can be overcome. Getting the upper hand on our problems is so much better than having problems rule over us! With freedom from sin, we are free to love and serve, smile and give, rejoice and live! Sins that we harbor in our spirits can be brought safely to the harbor of repentance and unloaded today.

Many of us know what it's like to be written off in our sin, but we can also come to know what's it's like to be restored. Time alone will tell, and God will be there with his grace to help us find our faith in the desert. Grace will help us to turn from our sin, and to receive forgiveness. In time we can return from what we thought was an unproductive time in our Christian experience with a pure faith, a clear conscience, and a clean heart.

Time is the silver lining in our spiritual wilderness. Time aids love in bringing about our healing. Both are in God's hands.

There is a time for everything, and a season for every activity under heaven:

A time to be born and a time to die,
a time to plant and a time to uproot,
a time to kill and a time to heal,
a time to tear down and a time to build,
a time to weep and a time to laugh,
a time to mourn and a time to dance,
a time to scatter stones and a time to gather them,
a time to embrace and a time to refrain,
a time to search and a time to give up,
a time to keep and a time to throw away,
a time to tear and a time to mend,
a time to be silent and a time to speak,
a time to love and a time to hate,
a time for war and a time for peace.

He has made everything beautiful in its time. He has also set eternity in the hearts of men; yet they cannot fathom what God has done from beginning to end (Ecclesiastes 3:1–8, 11).

Whether we needed to forsake the futility of an empty heart, or we find our souls falling away from truth, God allows us separation from the things that are damaging to our faith. Jesus sometimes heals our disconnection from him through a time to separate ourselves from the things coming between God and us. Leaving behind a religious mindset and taking time to restore our souls after such error gives us freedom. It's a double-edged sword for our healing. Separation from former bondages—through separation from such bondages—heals our separation from Jesus. When Jesus delivers us from our former bondage to a dead theology and a cold-hearted attitude, we will be free to find our faith. Serving God in faith is not the same as trying to serve God from an image of faith. Walking in the truth, the life, and the way of Christ will free us from a self-righteous, works-oriented, and religious mindset. Grace will flow through us, leading us to walk by faith and offer the healing of forgiveness to others. Faith opens our hearts to the gift of forgiveness. Forgiveness opens our hearts to the gift of faith.

As we stop listening to the voices around us, and disregard the judgment of those who think we have fallen from grace, we will be ready to learn to receive and hear only the voice of the Lord. Let others think what they think; sometimes we are only sleeping spiritually so we can wake up renewed. Some experiences in life are only revealed to us after we have gone through them. Trust the Lord, and in his time, Jesus will bring our apparently dead faith back to life. We pray: *Heavenly Father, please touch our hurting souls. Awaken us with the wisdom to heal in body, mind, and spirit as you healed the daughter of Jairus. Open our ears to hear and learn from listening to your voice, that in spite of what anyone else thinks, Jesus, you know the details in our lives. Help us trust in you.*

> While Jesus was still speaking, some men came from the house of Jairus, the synagogue ruler. "Your daughter is dead," they said. "Why bother the teacher anymore?" Ignoring what they said, Jesus told the synagogue ruler, "Don't be afraid; just believe." … When they came to the home of the synagogue ruler, Jesus saw a commotion, with people crying and wailing loudly. He went in and said to them, "Why all this commotion and wailing? The child is not dead but asleep." But they laughed at him.
>
> After he put them all out, he took the child's father and mother and the disciples who were with him, and went in where the child was. He took her by the hand and said to her, "Talitha koum!" (Which means, "Little girl, I say to you, get up!") Immediately the girl stood up and walked around (she was twelve years old). At this they were completely astonished (Mark 5:35–36, 38–42).

God is calling us, "Talitha Koum"—little one, arise. Come back to life. Jesus wants to spare us from an early grave. He wants us to stop our fatalistic lack of faith and over thinking our situation. He wants people to quit looking at our life and our testimony like we are Jairus's dead child, laughing behind our back, and believing we are a lost cause. He wants us to arise in faith. He doesn't want us to listen to the whispers of others who have given up on us and stopped praying for us. Those who reason that there is no point in bothering Jesus on our behalf err in their unbelief. While those mourners spoke words of unbelief, we have lived in unbelief. We have even behaved in unbelief. But we do not have to live among the spiritually dead in unbelief any longer.

Close your eyes.... See Jesus there beside the little girl.... Feel your soul's longing.... Feel his touch upon her hand.... Listen to his command ... get up ... live ... breathe; pray deeply, silently ... breathe ... believe, God is calling your name.... Marvel at creation, and then, my friend ... calmly feel the Spirit of God stirring, and know that he will raise you up to stand in your faith. *Today, if you hear his voice, let him soften every beat of your heart.*

If the whisperings of yesterday are still haunting you, and you still feel stuck today, and can't even think about tomorrow, relax.

> It is God who arms me with strength and makes my
> way perfect (Psalm 18:32).

It is the work of God to strengthen and perfect our faith. It is His voice, *"Talitha koum!"* that returns our soul to life. On that day, the child woke up and found herself surrounded by loving people who were astonished by her awakening to life. Isn't that our desire, too? We want to be alive spiritually and be a source of marvelous joy for others.

In the meantime, we must be considerate of our soul. Maybe we have not had enough time in the desert or have not gone there yet. No matter what our struggle, God's grace gives us permission to release ourselves from our confused and angry inner critic. Rest in his care, stay on his timetable, and let him do whatever is necessary to help us in our search for our faith. God knows our souls and what it will take to heal us. It certainly doesn't feel right to be left on a shelf for years on end, but he is not in a hurry about getting the job done. He is shaping our lives for eternity, and these few years we spend in the desert are a short span of time on his timetable. Whether we left our former faith in futility, or through falling away, the door of opportunity opened to us for finding a stronger faith by isolating ourselves from religious activity.

Maybe you never had such an experience, and maybe you never will. But just maybe, if you're honest, you will realize that a lot of souls around you were there yesterday, are there today, or will be there tomorrow. And maybe they need us to understand, maybe they need us to find them, or they need us to call them. Whatever you are thinking, I am only softly suggesting, from my spirit to yours: live the way God is calling you, according to your measure of faith. Get up! Live! Become the considerate, kind person you want to be. And while we're still living, let's do our gentle best to be merciful first to ourselves and then to all from the share of God's love we've been given.

Taking a little liberty with the passage from Ecclesiastes, here are some ideas for fine-tuning our faith in God. This might explain what it takes to heal and restore our faith. In time, our questions will have answers. But the questions are not what are important. What is important is our trust in God. Our faith grows when we accept the changes that happen over time to every purpose under heaven.

It is a time for a new faith to be born in your soul and for your old error to be left behind.

A time to plant a new faith and uproot the old one.

A time to kill off sin and find healing for your soul.

A time to tear down useless attitudes and build a new way of thinking.

A time to weep for your mistakes, and a time to laugh about what you learned.

A time to mourn for your old faith and dance with your new faith.

A time to scatter your faith and a time to gather it together.

A time to embrace parts of your faith and to refrain from other parts.

A time to search for a new life of faith and give up the old one.

A time to keep the truth and throw away the lies.

A time to tear out the disease and mend your heart back together.

A time to be silent and learn, and a time to speak and teach.

A time to love the good, and a time to hate the evil.

A time for war against dead religion and a time for peace in a faithful walk with God.

8

Traveling Toward Truth

on't blame other believers; blame the unbelief. So many people don't really know what they believe. You can spot them easily by this old adage, "What you know can be distinguished from what you believe by how you behave." Unfortunately, too many of us are living our lives in less than truthful thinking. We are like the blind Pharisees thinking we see, but we are blind. In order to see, we must travel toward the truth within to know in whom and what we believe and settle it forever in our hearts. As a man travels the world over, in search of what he needs, and returns home to find it, our faith awaits us. When it has all settled down and we come face-to-face with the truth, the final destination for us will be as A. W. Tozer said, "We are each one the result of every choice we've made." Therefore, we need to see to it that we make good choices in how we handle our faith.

> Leave them; they are blind guides. If a blind man
> leads a blind man, both will fall into a pit (Matt
> 15:14).

Whether by experience, or by tradition, if we willingly live our lives thinking we know something, and we don't bother to figure out if the creed we live and the prayers we recite have personal meaning, then we will surely be blind. We must know for certain that we are who we say we are, and our profession of faith and lifestyle approves what we believe. This is one reason to be grateful for a dry time spiritually. It will make you thirst for living water, and anything in your religious practice that doesn't quench your thirst will be revealed for what it is.

We simply must have a genuine, personal relationship with God. Anything less and we may only be offering lip service with our faith. Consider this question posed to Jesus:

> One of them, an expert in the law, tested him with this question: "Teacher, which is the greatest commandment in the Law?" Jesus replied, "Love the Lord your God with all your heart and with all your soul, and with all your mind." This is the first and greatest commandment (Matthew 22:35–38).

So many people equate their relationship with God to commitment to a church and or its leadership. Attending church and following the leaders is not the "all" in the commandment to love the Lord your God with all your heart and your neighbor as you love yourself. God desires that we relate to him with our whole heart, not half-heartedly. Corporate worship is only as genuine as the corporal body offering the worship, and it is not always a reliable source for getting through to God's heart, or for allowing him to speak individually to us. Our relationship with God and our worship of him requires that we focus our heart, mind, and soul on loving him every day. We must not give up our relationship with God for a relationship with our church or its leadership. We must search for truth.

If we traveled alongside Jesus as he went through his day, we would see that he had a lot of angst against the religious teachings of the scribes, teachers of the Law, and Pharisees. *Sadly, they had traded in their relationship with God for a religious system. Worse still, the things they taught put burdens on the believers, until they drove them away from God. The Pharisees' unbelief was detrimental to others. Their unmerciful judgments kept people bound in their sins, preventing them from feeling God's love.*

Jesus, wanting to reach every soul with the message of salvation, to put it glibly in keeping with his human side, let many people off the Pharisaical hook. The Pharisees did not like Jesus, the Son of God, usurping their authority and undermining their many, "The law states…" decrees! Religious men competed with works that Jesus through faith completed. They questioned everything Jesus did, and the challenge was on between them because Jesus didn't play by their manmade rules. Jesus traveled in mercy and truth. There are numerous accounts of the Pharisees trying to trap Jesus with their legalistic, controlling religion recorded in Matthew 12:10, Mark 12:13, Luke 11:53–54, and John 9:34. There is a distinct difference between the Pharisees' self-righteous administration of the Law and Jesus' understanding of the Law. Here is a classic example:

> The teachers of the law and the Pharisees brought in a woman caught in adultery. They made her stand before the group and said to Jesus, "Teacher, this woman was caught in the act of adultery. In the Law, Moses commanded us to stone such women. Now what do you say?" They were using this question in order to have a basis for accusing him. But Jesus bent down and started to write on the ground with his finger. When they kept questioning him, he straightened up and said to them, "If any one of you is without sin, let him be the first to throw a stone at her." Again he stooped down and wrote on the ground. At this, those who heard began to go away one at a time, the older ones first, until only Jesus was left, with the woman still standing there. Jesus straightened up and asked her, "Woman, where are they? Has no one condemned you?"
>
> "No one, sir," she said.
>
> "Then neither do I condemn you," Jesus declared. "Go now and leave your life of sin" (John 8:3–11).

Make no judgments about those exchanges. Jesus loved the Pharisees. He wept over Jerusalem. And even though the Pharisees and Religious leaders in his day were slightly egotistical and power tripping, Jesus did not go after them personally. *No, Jesus went after their unbelief and pointed out their sins of omission, their lack of mercy, and their false beliefs birthing wrong deeds.* In fact, in every encounter Jesus had with individuals, you see him speaking to them about the issues that were symptoms of their unbelief. Jesus' healing words of forgiveness went straight for the wound in people's souls. Jesus is the truth, and he knew that living in the truth of God's deliverance from sin is the only power that can set men free.

It is the lie in our belief system that keeps us in bondage to the oppression of our guilt. He did not come to condemn, but to save people from sins. The Samaritan woman was bound by the lies she believed to be the truth. Jesus asked the Samaritan woman for a drink, and she said, *"How can you a Jew, ask me a Samaritan for a drink?"* Didn't Jesus know that Jews do not associate with Samaritans? The Samaritan woman is an example of a person caught in a lifestyle of sin and bound to the conventions of her religious culture because she has no clue about the truth. Her confusion is evident in both her immoral lifestyle and her ignorance in believing that her religious training equates to having a relationship with and worshipping God. In her sin, she had no faith or ability to realize that she was actually in the presence of the Messiah. We also may miss out on being in his presence when we do not live in the truth.

> Jesus said to her (the Samaritan woman), "You are right when you say you have no husband. The fact is, you have had five husbands, and the man you now have is not your husband. What you have just said is quite true."
>
> "Sir," the woman said, "I can see that you are a prophet. Our fathers worshiped on this mountain, but you Jews claim that the place where we must worship is in Jerusalem."

"Believe me, woman, a time is coming when you will worship the Father neither on this mountain nor in Jerusalem. You Samaritans worship what you do not know; we worship what we do know, for salvation is from the Jews. Yet a time is coming and has now come when the true worshipers will worship the Father in spirit and in truth, for they are the kind of worshipers the Father seeks. God is spirit and his worshipers must worship in spirit and in truth."

The woman said, "I know that Messiah (called Christ) is coming. When he comes, he will explain everything to us."

Then Jesus declared, "I who speak to you am he" (John 4:18, 25–26).

The woman living in a pattern of sin was certainly an outcast in her society. However, Jesus did not judge her when he told her the truth. He set her free. She felt so affirmed that she went back to her town and shared the gospel of Jesus, the Messiah, and many people believed her. Jesus stayed for two days, and after hearing his words, many received their spiritual salvation and became believers. Are we any different from this woman in our need to stop our patterns of sinful thinking? Are we confused about how to have a relationship with God? What testimony do we give with our chosen lifestyle?

The woman had been five husbands into the path of darkness, but Jesus did not attack or condemn her. He lovingly confronted her with the truth and shed the light on her unbelief and hopeless lifestyle. She wanted to worship God and have a relationship with him, but she felt confused by her religious tradition regarding worship. Jesus helped this woman by pointing her to the root of her sin. Presently, He will help any one of us willing to listen to the truth to know for ourselves that these symptoms of sin revealed in immoral, impure, or otherwise unfulfilling lifestyles grow from the roots of our unbelief in Christ. We sin by discounting our worth.

The fact that Jesus traveled through Samaria was a cultural faux pas, since Jews didn't associate with Samaritans. However, Jesus, the living God, didn't live by the restrictions of the Jewish culture or rules of their religion. Jesus refused to adhere to rules that neglected our duty to value others. Jesus didn't follow the guidelines of the theology of that day because its focus was not on God's will for our lives. Of course, they ridiculed Jesus for associating with lower class sinners, but he did what was right in love showing the worth of every soul to God. He didn't blame the sinner; he blamed the unbelief that kept them in sin. Jesus led others to find their faith in God because he knew that without faith, it is impossible to please God.

> All the people saw this and began to mutter, "He has gone to be the guest of a sinner."
>
> Nevertheless, Zacchaeus stood up and said to the Lord, "Look, Lord! Here and now I give half of my possessions to the poor, and if I have cheated anybody out of anything, I will pay back four times the amount."
>
> Jesus said to him, "Today salvation has come to this house, because this man, too, is a son of Abraham. For the Son of Man came to seek and to save what was lost" (Luke 19:7–10).

Both the Samaritan woman and Zacchaeus were clearly lost and ostracized from the religious communities because of their choices to live in open sin. However, in response to Jesus' offer of redemption, they both repented and were set free from their guilt. Look at the change in Zaccheus. He stopped stealing and was willing to make restitution. That's what Jesus does when he saves us. His love cleans the slate and makes our spirits free to worship in truth. What about the sin in our lives? Have we lived a pattern of choices that are symptomatic of our unbelief? We, too, can let go of our sins, if we are ready to embrace the one who is seeking to save the virtue that was lost to us. Jesus has shown us that the redemption of every soul is of great value to God.

Those of us classified as "desert people, deserters of religion" may be able to identify with the Samaritan woman and her confusion about the proper place for worship. It is possible to have our theology all twisted up by the religion that promotes church attendance and minimizes the value of faith in Jesus. Are we living in truth and maintaining a right spirit so we can worship God in relationship to him as our Father? At times, we may have to admit that the lack in our ability to worship God stems from the limitations mutually imposed on us by personal sin, as well as our participation in a religious experience. We do well when we put our house in order on both accounts. Would God be pleased? provides our answers.

Fortunately, one thing we can learn as we travel in the desert is that our worship cannot be just a religious expression without faith. True worship cannot come from a heart harboring sin. When we come face-to-face with Jesus, we will come away with hearts overflowing with hope, repentance, peace and thanksgiving for the Lord. His gift of acceptance and healing forgiveness frees us to worship with our spirit set right by the truth. Just like the woman-at-the-well became a sister-in-Christ in tune with the truth, her spirit freed to worship, we can all become the kind of worshipers the Father seeks. Forsaking our unbelief, acknowledging the root of sin in our lives, and letting Jesus absolve us from our guilt offers us a chance to turn from our past. We can finally relate to God with our spirit in unity with his Spirit because our truth is in one accord with his truth.

If you are a true follower, there has to be a point when you want to live as genuinely as you can. *We have to become committed to our faith in Christ if we are going to give and receive everything meant for us to share with others during our physical life on this Earth.* We have to come face-to-face with Jesus, accept his grace, and renounce our sins. The only way we will ever really be who we are meant to be is to let Jesus explain everything to us. If the Samaritan woman had not spoken to Jesus, she would have died in sin and rejection, never having tasted the blessing of knowing the marvelous person God created her to be. Likewise, we need to stop being spiritual puppets, living by someone else's spin on faith. Instead, we need to start being spiritually earnest, living by what the word of God states is the truth. Jesus is the Word of God, the truth, and the life, and when we go to him, he will take us to that place of transparent honesty within our spirit. There we will learn what it means to worship, just as Jesus taught the Samaritan woman.

> Yet a time is coming and has now come when the true worshipers will worship the Father in spirit and truth, for they are the kind of worshipers the Father seeks. God is spirit and his worshipers must worship in spirit and in truth (John 4:23).

Most of us who have attended church, have, at some point in our lives, heard that the greatest sin of all is unbelief, or blasphemy against the Holy Spirit. Just think for a minute what the phrase "blasphemes against the Holy Spirit" indicates about how important it is to know the truth.

> I tell you the truth, all the sins and blasphemies of men will be forgiven them. But whoever blasphemes against the Holy Spirit will never be forgiven; he is guilty of an eternal sin (Mark 3:28–29).

In the past when my belief system crumbled, I was totally devastated, disillusioned, deluded, and dying. Literally, I even got cancer. Now I realize that my faith failed me, not only because I had not kept a clear conscience, and sinful attitudes harassed me, but mainly because I had not been practicing a faith of my own to begin with. Whoa, wasn't I a church leader, teacher, and worshiper? Yes, but I was living according to someone else's church program. I thought I was worshipping, but I was just sitting in the church, the place where the fathers of the church traditionally worshipped. The weekly bulletin, the songs from the choir, and the sermon from the preacher dictated most of our worship time. Even when I visited churches with lots of praise singing and worship, I couldn't give God what he desired. True worshipers worship in spirit and truth. I would think I had worshiped, but I would often walk away feeling empty. God and I just weren't able to commune and fellowship. That wasn't

God's fault. I was the one out of sync in the relationship. I was the one living in unbelief.

Moreover, we know that when one part of the body is disconnected or ailing, the whole body gets weak at the knees. We can be sure that we are not alone in our failure to hold on to our Head—Christ— from whom the whole body receives its nourishment. We may not realize the truth, but on any given Sunday, it is possible that many believers surrounding us may also be hanging loosely. People in our congregation may be totally unaware that they have not kept their focus and attention on worshipping God in spirit and truth.

The remedy is that we must look not only to our own interests but to the interest of others. Loving God is shown through loving others. Being rapt in a group mindset inadvertently may cause us to make certain individuals feel unworthy. We cannot be so caught up with pride and joy for our successfully active denomination and all our good works that we start sporting a congregational religion. If we do, we will end up worshipping the joy of being together in our success instead of taking our lives before God to offer praise and honor to him.

Why do we forget that we each stand alone before God when we come into his presence? Some of our church services do not even come near God's Spirit or truth because we think by virtue of our being present that we are faithfully worshipping God. Being in a large corporate worship service is the opposite of cultivating a faith that connects our hearts to God in true and spiritual worship. This is another reason our service for Christ is weak. Worship precedes ministry directed by the Holy Spirit and its emphasis is on taking care of every single sheep. Frankly, we are confused about the importance of each and every member of our congregation. We are too often in it for ourselves with blatant disregard for how to worship. We think that *where* we worship is the answer, but we neglect *how* and are as confused as was the Samaritan woman at the well. Where is our Christian awareness of spirit and truth? Jesus' wisdom heals our concepts of forgiveness, relationships, and worship.

Today, let's travel with Jesus and mend what seems to be true with the truth. Accepting God's forgiveness and obeying his word makes today a brand new day fresh with no mistakes in our itinerary. But listen very carefully to what we need to know before we move on. *If our faith falters or fails us by letting us fall flat on our face, then maybe it wasn't our faith at all.* Maybe we never really had the quality of faith God desires for us because we accepted what someone else told us as truth. Without questioning, we accepted the creed, or the theological perspectives and church covenants handed down by church leaders of the past. Today, we are asking God to search our hearts and to lead us into the truth. Even though we believe without a doubt that we had a genuine encounter with Jesus as a young person, when we stopped taking our cues from him, we started living according to someone else's idea of faithfulness.

Many of us lived a life full of spiritual acts we had been taught. However, for some of us, until we are driven into the desert where we can be alone with God, we may be unable to figure out the basis for our actions. We may have lived in the futility of acting like a Christian but not living as one. *Ultimately, we end up walking in unbelief because we do not know what we believe.* When we quit listening to God, we begin practicing a perfunctory religion. Allowing our hearts to take a vacation from the outward expression of our faith practices is nothing short of living in unbelief, and it leaves us feeling terribly empty inwardly.

As a small example of this, recently while visiting at a mainline denominational church, I witnessed the strangest thing during communion. The song leader seemed to be chewing the communion bread for a longer than necessary time. Suddenly I realized that she was chewing gum, even with the host in her mouth. Perfunctory religion can take us traveling away from the truth until what should be our best moments of worship become the worst. When we take communion it is in remembrance of Jesus, but if we don't know what we are remembering we might chew gum and eat the bread at the same time. Don't blame the believer, blame the unbelief.

All of us, at one time or another during our church services, have spent time vacationing in unbelief, separating our hearts from our faith practices. But if we let it go unchecked for too long it is that, which we do not realize that keeps us stagnating in a state of sin. For whatsoever is not of faith is sin. The challenge for us who want to travel toward the truth is to examine our itinerary. We must settle the issue regarding our doubts, setting aside the past regret of knowing all about God, but never believing in his desire to indwell our hearts. If we know we want to be with God, we have to map out a life of faith and pack into our lives what we need to get us there. In Matt. 25:3-4, the foolish ones took their lamps, but did not take any oil with them. The wise, however, took oil in jars along with their lamps.

We must make time along the route to study the Bible and spend time in the word of truth. No matter where we go or what we do, as we travel toward truth we need to be sure that our heart arrives at the destination as planned. *When we come to a place where our faith fails us, we will know that we have we neglected to pack the things we needed. How many years have we been traveling unprepared, and approving of things we do not actually approve of? Then we can be sure we are traversing in unbelief.* Nothing in your life is more important than knowing what you believe and traveling according to the truth in God's word. Replacing our doubts with a true faith in the author and finisher of our faith, Jesus Christ, the Son of God, will return love, joy, peace, and goodness to our hearts. We can be set free from the condemnation of sinful errors and learn not to blame the person who would like to be set free, but point the blame on the unbelief that keeps them held captive in sin. Instead, we should share our faith as we travel toward the truth.

> So whatever you believe about these things [eating, holy days, and drinking*] keep between yourself and God. Blessed is the man who does not condemn himself by what he approves. But the man who has doubts is condemned if he eats, because his eating is not from faith; and everything that does not come from faith is sin (Romans 14:22–23).
>
> * Bracketed phrase added by author

9

Sifting Through Shifting Sands ~ Finding Faith-Filled Friends

*A*nyone who has been away from the practice of a faith they once believed in knows what it is like to sift through the shifting sands. There are definitely many sandstorms to endure when you find yourself walking in the desert with your former belief system lying beneath your feet, no longer a shelter over your head. After all, some of us have firsthand experience with Jesus' words concerning the outcome of a faith built on shifting sand and not on solid rock.

> Therefore everyone who hears these words of mine and puts them into practice is like a wise man who built his house on the rock. The rain came down, the streams rose, and the winds blew and beat against that house; yet it did not fall, because it had its foundation on the rock. But everyone who hears these words of mine and does not put them into practice is like a foolish man who built his house on sand. The rain came down, the streams rose, and the

> winds blew and beat against that house, and it fell
> with a great crash (Matt 7:24–27).

This is not to cause further despair for us, but it only directs us to the truth that we need to know in order to live the life of faith that stands the tests of time. The teachings of Jesus are the bedrock for a faithful life. The daily practice of Jesus' teachings in our lives is the attribute of wisdom. Apply it this way. What we do every day of our lives determines whether we are building a rock-solid life or we are just shifting around buckets of sand. "But everyone who hears these words of mine and does not put them into practice is like a foolish man who built his house on sand."

Faith comes by hearing the Word of God and grows by practicing the principles in the Word of God. Thinking back to the places we left prior to our being stranded and feeling forsaken in the desert, we might find that we did not have the proper support to sustain our faith. Had we been in a three-strand cord of fellowship with the Lord, his Word, and faith-filled friends, we would have been able to steer faithfully around the crisis. A friendship in Christ provides the love and encouragement we need to practice our faith (his words).

The first step in finding faithful friends is becoming a faith-filled person. I hope that your experience and time in seeking to become a better person has given you insight and conviction to understand the measure of faith you have received. You need to know your faith like you know yourself. Being committed to walking by faith usually puts us on the path with others who feel the same way. It's joyful to walk along the path with friends. After spending so long working through the failed faith and lack of good friendships that were part of the completely awful past, the things we have learned about our souls and other souls should enable us to set sail on our rebuilt ship of faith. Just let the Spirit of God breathe the wind of love into our sails. Through our trust and silent prayers, he charts a course to guide us to honest and likeminded people of faith.

When I was a little girl, my Catholic grandmother, Gram Hope, had a St. Christopher statue on the dashboard of her red Rambler station wagon and a string of rosary beads hanging from the rearview mirror. Every day that we got into Gram's car, before she even turned the key in the ignition, she would say, "Say 'thank God for another day,' Tammy." Then she would start the car and smile at me, saying, "Today is our today." Gram gave me other things that are still part of my measure of faith, like caring for strangers, volunteering in the Neighborhood House, offering blessings before every meal, and saying prayers of confession and petitions for blessing others before sleeping at night.

Besides that, Gram made every day about helping people. Many of those trips we took in her little Rambler were to houses of widows who lived in areas about the city of Cincinnati. Neighborhood communities at that time were related by ethnicity. Gram had Italian, Irish, Jewish, Black, and German friends. Several days a week, Gram would drive one of these women to the market, the doctor, the bank, the hairdresser, or anywhere else she needed to go. I realize now what a service she was providing to her friends back in those days. Many women born before or at the turn of the nineteenth century didn't learn to drive and didn't have the independence of Gram, born in 1898. By today's standards, it may not seem like an extraordinary walk of faith, but the services and friendship Gram offered to widows was priceless. Thinking of Gram's ministry helps me understand what it means to be a friend who shares the faith in her heart.

> Religion that God our Father accepts as pure and faultless is this: to look after orphans and widows in their distress and to keep oneself from being polluted by the world (James 1:27).

These memories of my Christian grandmother are so indelibly impressed on my heart that I am forever seeking and seeing the forlorn and needy. Sometimes, the love of God and the example of faith I saw in Gram wells up in me, and I find it in my heart to reach out in whatever way I can. This happens to all of us when we avail ourselves to the promptings of the Holy Spirit within. Gram was truly the salt of the Earth; the light in her life was practical, while her infectious outgoing joy provided help to lighten the load of others. She lived each day thankfully, according to the measure of her faith, and she practiced it through her works.

> But someone will say, "You have faith; I have deeds."
> Show me your faith without deeds, and I will show
> you my faith by what I do (James 2:18).

One of the benefits of our desert experience is that it will drive us to realize the one question that we simply must ask ourselves. Like the parable of the talents, are we using our measure of faith and increasing it, or hiding it away under some bowl? At some point, I began to understand that the longing that sent me into the desert to begin with was the personal quest to find answers to the questions I needed to know regarding my faith.

What was I doing to show my faith? How was I keeping sinfulness from polluting my faith? Was my testimony remaining salty, so that I, like Gram, could consider myself the salt of the Earth?

Sometimes, going into a time of soul searching is the only way to find what's in our hearts. There are questions we each must ask in order to settle our hearts with faith. For example, ask yourself, What is the just way to measure one's individual gift of faith? What is my working definition of faith? Do I understand the way to keep my faith alive? What does the Bible teach about faith? Am I ready and willing to face the decisive test to start showing daily my faith through deeds? Like those who once touched our hearts with the disciples' faith, we are to reach out to others to draw men to faith in Jesus. Sharing the light of the gospel and its truth with others makes us the salt of the Earth. Jesus related that the things we do to show our faith is salt and light for the world. We know that we all need these elements to live, and Jesus equates what we do as life sustaining deeds. Are we ready and willing to cultivate the active kind of faith that shows itself in love for others?

Over time, we may begin to realize the biggest hindrance to our faith is in answering the questions. What do I believe about the Son of God? Who would I say he is? This would, of course, determine whether or not we are willing to share our testimony. We must have faith if we are going to share it with others. For those of us who know

God and believe we have a relationship with Jesus, many times we fail to share our faith because either our faith is too weak or we feel ashamed of something within. If so, we would do well to ask, Am I ashamed of the gospel of Christ or just ashamed of myself? *The fact is,* for those of us who know that we have a genuine faith, if we are embarrassed to take a stand for the gospel of Christ, the root is shame. Either we are ashamed of the Lord, or we are ashamed because of sin within ourselves. When we are feeling guilty and condemned, we are denying the gift of our salvation, which is the forgiveness of our sins. Sin is the only thing that has the power to make us feel inferior or inadequate. *If we are ashamed of ourselves, then we are ashamed of the gospel of Christ.* The issue of our worth was settled forever when Jesus provided us healing from our sin through the forgiveness of sins. He honors us with worthiness as his children and bestows peace within our hearts. *Forgiveness is a mustard seed of faith which grows daily leading us to likeminded, spiritual friends.*

Consider how gently and persistently Jesus took the needed time to restore Peter through forgiveness after Peter had denied Him.

> Simon son of John, do you truly love me more than these? (John 21:15–17)

Jesus was helping Peter let go of the loneliness caused by his shame for past sins. Sin had made Peter feel unworthy and cut off from the Lord. It took Peter time to realize that Jesus wanted to embrace him with love, not chastisement for his failing. Jesus wanted Peter to accept his forgiveness and to forgive himself. Jesus wanted to fully restore Peter to his faith. Peter had experienced sorrow when his faith failed. *This is extremely important for us to grasp, because faith in Christ can only begin when we embrace the gospel of Christ and receive forgiveness for our sins through faith. Peter was not able to begin his ministry to feed the sheep or lead others to the Savior until he was restored to Jesus after his denial of Christ. Sin has a way to make the soul shrivel up and cut itself off from others. Jesus knew that Peter would not stop feeling the shame until he first stopped feeling alone and cut off from God's love and acceptance.*

We are no different from Peter. We can only walk by faith when we are not ashamed of the gospel of Christ or ashamed of the sins in our past. The gospel offers the power of forgiveness and salvation to all who believe. One only has to remember how many times the Lord accompanied his healing miracles with the words, "Thy sins are forgiven." If we want our faith back, or we want it to grow, we cannot allow ourselves to indulge in self-pity or shame. We must be able to claim, "I am not ashamed of the gospel of Christ."

> You are the salt of the earth. But if the salt loses its saltiness, how can it be made salty again? It is no longer good for anything, except to be thrown out and trampled by men. You are the light of the world. A city set on a hill cannot be hidden. Neither do people light a lamp and put it under a bowl. Instead they put it on its stand, and it gives light to everyone in the house. In the same way, let your light shine before men, that they may see your good deeds and praise your Father in heaven (Matthew 5:13–16).

This reminds me of the time I asked Gram if she had it all to do over again, would she do it the same, sins and all? I was shocked when Gram said, "Yes, I'd do it all again exactly the same way. God gave me my life, and everything in it brought me closer to him. Have faith in God, sweetie, and everything will be all right." I get it now. It doesn't matter where I failed. God held on to me. He shaped my faith through my trials. He is still God, and we are still his. So just like Gram said, "Today is our today. Thank God for another day." And we do thank God for another day. God will take care of our faith. He will put us back at the helm. Gram had no regrets for her failures. She did not place the blame on others, and she always kept her conscience clear. Daily she prayed to God for a pure heart and a right spirit. She didn't condemn herself or others for sin. She lived this scripture.

> Do not judge, and you will not be judged. Do not condemn, and you will not be condemned. Forgive,

and you will be forgiven. Give and it will be given to you. A good measure, pressed down, shaken together and running over, will be poured into your lap. For with the measure you use, it will be measured to you (Luke 6:37).

We need to stop wandering alone in our judgment of ourselves and others. We need to stop cutting ourselves off and step back from the anger and the disillusionment. The disturbance of the past has tossed us to and fro upon the waves of being too strict on ourselves and others. Jesus has asked us to let him love us and wants us to know without any doubt that we love him, too. He is our faithful friend. If we are harboring anger, we will be a religious wreck. Look what happens to us when we judge and accuse.

You have heard that it was said to the people long ago, "Do not murder, and anyone who murders will be subject to the judgment." But I tell you that anyone who is angry with his brother will be subject to judgment. Again, anyone who says to his brother, "Raca," is answerable to the Sanhedrin. But anyone who says, "You fool!" will be in danger of the fire of hell. Therefore, if you are offering your gift at the altar and there remember that your brother has something against you, leave your gift there in front of the altar. First go and be reconciled to your brother; then come and offer your gift. Settle matters quickly with your adversary who is taking you to court. Do it while you are still with him on the way, or he may hand you over to the judge, and the judge may hand you over to the officer, and you may be thrown into prison. I tell you the truth, you will not get out until you have paid the last penny (Matthew 5: 21–26).

It's so much easier to lay it down, and put it behind, when we simply confess it to God and ask him to forgive us. The good news is that the last penny is paid through our repentance and Jesus' atonement. When we grasp this, we will understand why Gram could say she would do it all the same way. Jesus made her worthy. She knew the secret of faith. She learned as a faithful seeker that we are genuinely free to live a life of faith in the presence of other faithful believers. In the heat of the trial, we worry that we will be in the desert of banishment forever. But the day is at hand for us to leave the desert behind. Faith and faithful friends will make us capable of connecting in fellowship with other genuine and likeminded believers

One day, we may actually be ready to follow the Lord when he leads us to attend and join a church family. Our prayers for guidance, our willingness to step out where he leads, and our obedience to follow will protect us from going someplace, or any old place under compulsion. The Holy Spirit will never force us. He invites us to follow him with our hearts in tune. We will not find him leading us to do anything with an empty heart. He guards our hearts through praise and prayer. Prayer is communion with God through the Holy Spirit. He will lead us in truth if we will follow him in faith. The practice of faith is to worship in spirit and truth from sincere and forgiven hearts. Worship before an eternal God in communion with the Holy Spirit will connect our hearts to God and fill us with his grace and peace. Gratitude for our creator God and Jesus our Savior expands our faith and prompts us to love and serve others in the family of God. True worship will lead us to minister to God by caring for and meeting the needs of others. We will do more than give God lip service when we obey his teachings from our hearts.

> You hypocrites! Isaiah was right when he prophesied about you: "These people honor me with their lips, but their hearts are far from me. They worship me in vain; their teachings are but rules taught by men" (Matthew 15:7–9).

No, the path of the hypocrite is not for us. When we start searching for faith-filled friends, we cannot, nor can they be among those who only pay lip service to God. We need friends whose hearts are honest, and whose lifestyle practices are upright before God and man. Another way we offer worship to God is through ministry. As we look in the scripture, we see the inspiration of Jesus chosen, faithful friends allowed them to follow Jesus wholeheartedly. They left their nets and followed Jesus because they wanted to minister alongside him. That inspired kind of faith is what we need to share in our friendships.

Jesus looked for goodhearted men to help him fulfill God's promise to redeem mankind. God has a wonderful way of giving us a body of friends to help us to renew our faith. The Holy Spirit draws us together and prompts us to pray for one another. In this way a body of believers is able to stand and administer the gifts of the Holy Spirit to the fold.

By giving us a group of faithful friends, God helps us to straighten out our thinking and put our priorities in order. As the Proverb says, "As iron sharpens iron, so doth a man sharpen his friend." Jesus said we are his friends if we do the things he says to do. The things he says to do consist of our ministry to love God and our neighbor. Service and ministry are awaiting us, and we must find others willing to walk alongside us to fulfill our calling. In the past, our friends may have been too involved in their own lives or lived too far away, or were not interested to spend time praying, studying, or ministering. They were not like the inspired friends of Jesus who left all to follow him. We need the kind of friends who will stay with us and sharpen us when we get dull. For some, the reason the shipwreck hurt us so much is that we may not have developed supportive friendship with believers who came along side and pointed us back to God when the storms of life battered our ship. Except for the grace of God, there we would be, but instead here we are. Today is our today and this is our time to say, "I will begin anew."

We are going to start anew learning from Jesus how to find a couple of good friends. Observe how Jesus found four of his friends and listen to the words He spoke to them. This might actually help us in our search for a support system. And trust me, we all need a support system if we are going to stand strong and live the worthwhile kind of life God purposed for us. The first two found by Jesus were Peter and his brother, Andrew.

> As Jesus was walking beside the Sea of Galilee, he saw two brothers, Simon called Peter and his brother Andrew. They were casting a net into the lake, for they were fishermen. "Come follow me," Jesus said, "and I will make you fishers of men." At once they left their nets and followed him (Matthew 4:18-20).

The second two, James and John, were also anglers and brothers.

> Going on from there, he saw two other brothers, James, son of Zebedee, and his brother, John. They were in a boat with their father, Zebedee, preparing their nets. Jesus called them, and immediately they left the boat and their father and followed him (Matthew 4:21–22).

What we know about these four men from this scripture is that they were all fishermen and Jesus called them while they were busy at their jobs. They were interested in Jesus and dropped everything to follow him. Andrew was already acquainted with Jesus through John the Baptist and knowing that he was referred to as the Lamb of God by John the Baptist provided his inspiration to follow Jesus.

> The next day John was there again with two of his disciples. When he saw Jesus passing by, he said, "Look, the Lamb of God!"
>
> When the two disciples heard him say this, they followed Jesus. Turing around, Jesus saw them following and asked, "What do you want?"
>
> They said, "Rabbi" (which means teacher), "where are you staying?"
>
> "Come," he replied, "and you will see."

So they went and saw where he was staying and spent that day with him. It was about the tenth hour.

Andrew, Simon Peter's brother, was one of the two who heard what John had said and who followed Jesus. The first thing Andrew did was to find his brother Simon and tell him, "We have found the Messiah" (that is, the Christ). And brought him to Jesus (John 1:35–42).

I am not saying your friends should be fishermen; your friends should be interested in Jesus and willing to follow alongside him. Jesus saw purity in their hearts and intuitively knew they were honest men seeking to live right. Friendship must be reciprocated, based on common values, and mutually uplifting. Jesus knew these men would be able to receive his blessing and to pass it on to others. Our friendships should take us closer to God. We need friends with whom we can share Jesus and friendships that keep Jesus at the center of all our interactions. When Jesus called his disciples, he called them to this one purpose, to join him in becoming fishers of men. He wants us to do the same, to become those friends of his who bring others to Him. The focus was and is on Jesus' purpose to bring salvation and light to our lives and to the lives of all as "fishers of men."

One thing we can agree on in our shared humanity is that all of us will go through trials of life. When a trial comes to us, there is nothing short of genuine faith that will enable us to stand hopeful through prayer and stay strong in spirit. If we had not gone through any trials with disease, rebellious children, unfaithfulness, rejection, unbelief, and abandonment, we would not have learned anything in the desert. In fact, if our lives had been free from the storms of life, and unhappy confrontations with Pharisees along the way, we might not have thirsted for living water or hungered for the bread of life. In that we might not have found God at all.

We are not experiencing anything uncommon to man if we have lost sight of our faith for a while and have hidden our life in the desert. The desert is a place of learning and growth. Walking on those hot, shifting sands makes us want to feel the solid rock under our feet again. Regardless of how we are beguiled, buffeted, or belittled during the sandstorms of life, hearing the words of Jesus and putting those principles into practice will restore us. Putting God's word into practice with a tested and true faith will help us build our lives on a solid foundation and put our emotions on a stable course.

For many of us, the sands have slipped through the hourglass, completing our time of learning in the desert. For those who are not ready to move forward in faith, take courage and look to the Lord to make provisions for you during this season of adjustment. The Lord lovingly allows each person the time needed to heal from a hurting heart, while protecting a wavering faith. Even though the isolation seems senseless, there is a time to every purpose under heaven. God has a purpose to everything and he promises that he will use all of our trials to bring about something good in our lives.

As the Apostle Paul wrote:

> And we know that in all things God works for the good of those who love him, who have been called according to his purpose (Romans 8:28).

Unbeknownst to us, during our solitary and lonely time in our spiritual desert, Jesus is with us. It is God's will that we hear his words. God will not go back on his will to anyone who listens when Jesus calls, "Come follow me." He will not abandon you or banish you from his presence when you seek him. *He understands why you are confused or feeling forsaken, and if you will look to him, he will teach you the things you need to know to give you the faith you long to have.* God's love is always our protection when we temporarily feel rejection. We can place our trust in God, knowing that he will always be willing and available to protect our calling and strengthen our faith. Remember yesterday, today, and tomorrow, for where but there will we find our meaning? Yesterday, today, and tomorrow, Jesus is the Christ who calls us to repent, restores our faith, and offers us his protection when upsetting events set us apart.

The excerpt below from Luke contains a portion of the same truth found in the book of Matthew. One of the most beautiful spiritual lessons you can study is in the Beatitudes, given through the Sermon on the Mount as recorded in Matthew Chapter 5. Nothing written on Earth can touch the spirit of the inner man as profoundly as these words of Jesus. They are words spoken in love through the authority of the Holy Spirit, which will encourage, strengthen, and guide you no matter how high the temperature in your desert rises. After you have finished reading here, I hope you will finish with this blessing in faith to read firsthand the words of Jesus recorded in the fifth chapter of the book of Matthew. Give special attention to the first eleven verses, because they are written about us. *Practice prayer, keep your conscience clear, and keep God near.*

> And without faith it is impossible to please God, because anyone who comes to him must believe that he exists and that he rewards those who earnestly seek him (Hebrews 11:6).

Here are the Beatitudes we find in Luke's gospel:

> He went down with them and stood on a level place. A large crowd of his disciples was there and a great number of people from all over Judea, from Jerusalem, and from the coast of Tyre and Sidon, who had come to hear him and to be healed of their diseases. Those troubled by evil spirits were cured, and the people all tried to touch him, because power was coming from him and healing them all. Looking at his disciples, he said:

> "Blessed are you who are poor, for yours is the kingdom of God.

> Blessed are you who hunger now, for you will be satisfied.

> Blessed are you who weep now, for you will laugh.

> Blessed are you when men hate you, when they exclude you and insult you, and reject your name as evil, because of the Son of Man.
>
> Rejoice in that day and leap for joy, because great is your reward in heaven. For that is how their fathers treated the prophets." Luke 6:17–23

Consider Jesus' call to us as his faith-filled friends, "Come follow me." We must commit to be genuine, to be who we are meant to be, cultivating within others and ourselves the greatest three. The keys to Jesus' ministry are found in the authority of our faith, hope, and love. With the power of these virtuous gifts, we may bring others to share in the privilege of becoming God's children.

> Then Jesus came to them and said, "All authority in heaven and on earth has been given to me. Therefore, go and make disciples of all nations, baptizing them in the name of the Father and of the Son and of the Holy Spirit, and teaching them to obey everything I have commanded you. And surely I am with you always, to the very end of the age" (Matthew 28:18–20).

Epilogue ~ What We Need to Know to Set Sail Again and Serve God

*S*o how do we recover from a shipwrecked faith? How do we set sail again? Our first step is to acknowledge that faith is a gift from God, just as life is a gift, and embrace it with thanksgiving. All honest hearts know that we never have a life that is not a gift. From the moment of conception, we are recipients of life from an unseen miracle. After our birth, we continue to receive the breath of life from the same unseen miracle. Our gifts are not just a physical life and talents; by faith, we receive spiritual life and fruits. The spiritual qualities enable us to use our physical gifts and talents for God. Using our gifts and talents as a means for blessing is exactly what Jesus did.

Therefore, when the crisis comes or your faith fails, you will certainly not want to say how unfair it all was. Anyone who has ever been disgruntled over their circumstances has probably lamented the proverbial "Why me?" Maybe we should say, "Why not me?" Obviously, these questions validate our being angry with God. We wonder what we did to deserve unfair treatment to experience a test. Excuse me; do you think that Jesus never experienced a test? Of course he was tested, and the tests will come to every living human being on this planet because each of us has a free will to make choices. We will participate in the trials of life, and our response will be a choice between good and evil, the spiritual nature or the carnal lifestyle. Just rejoice in the acceptance that through our trials in life, God gives us many opportunities to have our faith tested, so that our false beliefs will surface.

If we want to get off the shoreline and set sail again, we have to stop all such whining over the trials we encounter. If we choose sin, we will fail the tests. Furthermore, if we choose to live by the sinful nature, we will not be able to use our gift of life or our talents and abilities for God. In fact, we may end up like the servant who hid his talent and presented it unused to the master, on the day of his return. The master was not pleased to see the servant had neglected his gift. Understanding that we have the indwelling Holy Spirit to provide daily guidance helps us to understand that we must make a choice to live by the Spirit.

> So I say, live by the Spirit, and you will not gratify the desires of the sinful nature. For the sinful nature desires what is contrary to the Spirit and the Spirit what is contrary to the sinful nature. They are in conflict with each other, so that you do not do what you want. But if you are led by the Spirit, you are not under the law (Galatians 5:16–18).

If we are going to keep our faith intact and not experience a shipwrecked faith, we must be doing what God created us to do as Paul advised Timothy, "Hold on to the prophecies made about you." Our calling and the work meant for us in this life is a spiritual gift. We cannot neglect our ordained work, but we must not do our work with a carnal spirit. If we start relying only on our natural abilities to serve God, that will only cause us to have a self-promoting pride. We can only accomplish God's work through our spiritual nature, and we must rely on the guidance of the Holy Spirit. *We have to fight our flesh to fight for our faith.* We need to live in a way that allows us to grow and develop the fruits of the spirit placed within by God.

> But the fruit of the Spirit is love, joy, peace, patience, kindness, goodness, faithfulness, gentleness and self-control. Against such things there is no law.

> Those who belong to Christ Jesus have crucified the sinful nature with its passions and desires. Since we live by the Spirit, let us keep in step with the Spirit. Let us not become conceited, provoking and envying each other (Galatians 5: 22–26).

Have you ever found yourself feeling depressed, alone, out on the shoals, shipwrecked, a failure in your own eyes, questioning your worth and pleading, *what do I do now?* If we are willing to be honest, we can easily figure out which of those acts of the sinful nature tripped us up, and which of those virtues will put our boat back on the water. When our belief system has been banked, and we realize our faith is not working, it's time to monitor our thinking. When faced with having to choose between our way or God's way of seeing things, we would be wise to choose the spiritual. Consider the difference between our sinful nature and the nature of the Holy Spirit. Here is the clue to keeping our faith in the right condition for service. We need to renounce our part in sin.

> The acts of the sinful nature are obvious: sexual immorality, impurity and debauchery; idolatry and witchcraft; hatred, discord, jealousy, fits of rage, selfish ambition, dissensions, factions, and envy; drunkenness, orgies, and the like. I warn you, as I did before, that those who live like this will not inherit the kingdom of God (Galatians 5:19–21).

None of us wants to admit we may be guilty of sin held in our thinking or harbored in our hearts. There are only two choices in response to our shortcomings—hardness or humility. I often have to look within myself to check how I respond to my sin and failures. I know I can choose pride and hide a lot of mistakes. However, mistakes that we try to hide cling to our souls like plastic wrap and suffocate all the goodness in us. Our well-being and our integrity suffer when we choose pride instead of humility. Jesus offers grace to the humble. Choose grace. *Humility is not only a beautiful garment to cover yourself with during times of trouble but is the fertilizer of the soil from which a strong tree of life grows to produce fruit of peace and other virtues in your character.*

Virtues are evidence of a relationship with the one true God who resides within every soul yielded to the Holy Spirit of God. We find whether our character is virtuous when we face the test of adversity or temptation to sin. If our ship (testimony of faith) ends up wrecked, then we can be sure we have failed the test, but glad for the revelation that we are lacking in faith. A test failed gives us an opportunity to improve our souls. A test of faith shows us what we believe and can reveal what motivates us. If our motivations are for something other than following God's will, a test will open our souls, purify, and refine the belief in our hearts. We may be surprised to find what's lacking in our spirit. *A test is a gift that opens the way for us to find a true faith in the one true God.*

Faith grows stronger during testing, and it exposes the level of your commitment. If you allow God, he will strengthen you during and after each right or wrong choice you make. He loves you always, even if you fail to respond in a righteous manner. As long as your will is placed, through faith, in his hands, God will keep you close to him and guide you to safety during the unpredictable storms in your life. Jesus always chose to do the Father's will and shows us that, through prayer, we too can have a faithful relationship with our Father. He lived such a life here on Earth with us.

All this talk about humility and virtue points us to becoming a person of earnest faith like Jesus. When he experienced testing by the people opposed to him, he had to make choices to respond as God desired. He is the Good News, because in each case, he chose to allow the Father within to strengthen, help, and encourage everyone around him. During each miracle or parable he taught, he chose to do the will of the Father, not taking any credit for his part in doing well, but pointing everyone to look in the direction of the Father in heaven, from whom every worthwhile message and perfect help comes. The miracles that Jesus performed were gifts from the Father. Jesus and the Father acted in one accord to perform every miracle.

> Jesus answered, "Don't you know me, Philip, even
> after I have been among you such a long time?

Anyone who has seen me has seen the Father. How can you say, 'Show us the Father'?' Don't you believe that I am in the Father, and that the Father is in me? The words I say to you are not just my own. Rather, it is the Father, living in me, who is doing his work. Believe me when I say that I am in the Father and the Father is in me; or at least believe on the evidence of the works themselves. Very truly I tell you, whoever believes in me will do the works I have been doing, and they will do even greater things than these, because I am going to the Father" (John 14:9–12).

Jesus claimed no goodness within himself, but he clearly stated that whatever we see that is good in him, it is only a reflection of the Father. Jesus, indwelt by the Holy Spirit, clearly loved God with his entire heart, mind, and will, and he displayed the transparent love of the Father to his fellow human beings. Jesus gladly allowed God to be in charge of his life and work through him while he communed with him daily. In living his way, Jesus never had to experience a shipwrecked faith.

In addition, Jesus, unlike religious leaders, prophets, or teachers from the culture of his day, wanted us to know that God is the only being capable of being entirely holy. When we trust in Jesus, he takes away powerful feelings of self-sufficient pride and self-condemnation until we understand that without him, our human attempt to live a holy life is inadequate. He offers us a holy life, if we will relinquish our desires to the Holy Spirit and let the life of the spirit of God live through us. A life yielded to the love of God within is the only life that can come anywhere close to holy. Even in that, all human beings will still have times of failure. We must embrace that the spirit of God is willing, but our flesh is weak and often chooses what pleases us in the physical part of life. What is physical is not of faith. Faith is the work of the Holy Spirit within who leads us to uphold the will of God. A misunderstanding of this principle often leads to a shipwreck of our faith.

Religiosity fails to keep this strand of truth pure, that it is not our determination, but God's Holy Spirit who brings goodness out of our soul. Religion void of genuine faith wants us to believe that we can make ourselves godly by running effective programs, or earning honor for religious achievements. A religious ideology may make us believe that we will earn rewards for our sacrifices, but what we do when we try to live by the letters of a manmade religious guideline is not borne from the will of a holy and omnipotent God. Its source is from a traditional custom or false doctrine. If we don't abandon this self-centered thinking, we will not be able to set sail and serve God in faith.

Jesus also warns us to beware of false prophets and teachers (see Matt 7:15) who steal God's glory and divide it amongst themselves to promote their agendas. Being deceived within, they think nothing of using spiritual authority in selfish, religious attempts to gain something from God. Their feel good teachings and positive messages distort God's word. They lead their followers to seek after God for the bounty of his blessings, for the soothing of their emotions, but not for the righteousness of Christ.

Although modern feel good, prosper, and enjoy life sermons have left dead, manmade traditions, they have replaced them with a new doctrine. They teach reverence for God based on what reward we can earn when we revere him. Note any doctrine we profess that does not produce the fruit of the spirit of truth will drive our faith off its course. Religion that makes the focus of this earthly life the goal of its followers has taken their eyes, ears, and hearts away from Jesus. How conveniently we have forgotten to preach the truth found in 1John 2:15:

> Do not love the world. If anyone loves the world or anything in the world, the love of the Father is not in him. For everything in the world, the cravings of sinful man, the lust of his eyes and the boasting of what he has and does are not from the Father, but from the world.

The worldly mindset prevalent in spiritual circles today is similar to the hype held among the religious elite in biblical days. God blessed me, but God cursed you attitudes were pervasive among the religious whose holier than thou and legalistic traditions replaced sound doctrine. Think of the Pharisee's prayer (Luke 18:9-14) thanking God that he was not like the sinner who was praying in church beside him. Or the disciples (John 9:1-3) who showed disdain for the blind man when they asked Jesus if the man's sin or his parents' sin had caused him to be born blind. Consider the parable of the rich man and Lazarus (Luke 16:19-25). What sound doctrine of religion would promote spiritual pride, disdain those less fortunate, and hoard wealth in the face of obvious need?

Yet, isn't this similar to the new legalism by which we measure our faith? We think our spiritual understanding is superior so we look down on other sinners. We think people who struggle with infirmities or depression deserve them as a result of sin, and we amass fortunes and feel entitled to keep them for ourselves.

Do we now boast when we succeed in making our lives richer than those of others? Is our rich man vs. Lazarus lifestyle something for which we strive? There is no excuse if we replace our love for God and our respect for Christ's cross with things that we taut as status symbols of God's spiritual favor? Are we guilty of making this the Lord's goal for man? God's will is not to prove his blessings by our proud practice of manipulating spiritual laws on giving and receiving. On many fronts, the preaching of the gospel has been watered down to the good news of our spiritual success stories, and our personal good fortune. Jesus warns us in (Matthew 10:38, 16:24, & Luke 14:27) to pick up our cross, to deny ourselves, and to follow him.

It is not God's sole purpose in redemption to glorify men. He takes care of our needs in response to our prayers, and as his children, we are the recipients of his forgiveness and his blessings. But the glory in which we boast belongs to him. He calls us to carry our cross and to become Christ like. The gospel of Jesus Christ is a gospel of eternal salvation, not a gospel of earthly exaltation.

What is the most important thing we need to know to set sail again and serve God? What we need, above everything else we hear on the airwaves, is to know the voice of the Good Shepherd. What we need is to only hear, and to only follow, his voice, and his teaching. Because obeying Jesus' teaching is the only way to serve the Father.

Thoughts for Fun!
Faith is Superior to Religion

Dearest Reader:

I wrote the following statements one sleepless night in my desert. They are my original ideas, and although there is a grain of truth in each, they are just for fun. Indirectly linked to the underlying premise for this book, each idea attests that faith in Christ is superior to religion.

Yours truly,
Tamara Kent

Help Me! I'm a Religious Wreck and You Can Find Me in the Desert.

Sometimes you have to go to war with your religion in order to find your faith.

The shelter from a bad religion is in the desert seeking faith.

Religion is the opium of the hypocrites. Faith is the joy of the redeemed.

Religiosity stifles the curiosity of children.

Religion is a blind form of faith.

Religion does not relate—it rules.

Faith is the overthrow of religious overtures.

Jesus is the fulfillment of the law, and he accomplished this through the spirit.

Religion is a setup. Religion was a setup by man to set a man up to set him up, or to cast man down to cast him down. Anyway you look, it looks like a trap.

The desert heat is better for finding true faith than the cold conditions found in many churches.

The combined consciousness of carnal minds is an accurate description of many church committees.

If your faith shipwrecked, maybe it was because you had a collision with the icebergs running the church.

Repentance from a religious mindset is the first step to finding your faith in God.

Much too often, faith is replaced by religion once you are baptized and listed on the church roster.

Religion has its own reality show, and you can check it out on Sunday morning.

Religion has lost the elementary principles of faith and replaced it with working in church programs.

The elementary principles of religious organizations make faith a secondary requirement of membership.

The prerequisite for finding true faith in God is to get burned by religion.

When a man forsakes the futility of a false religion because he wants more of God, the fakers say he has fallen away, but God knows he is really on his way to finding true faith.

Finding faith in the desert is not a new idea; God started using it for training Moses, and after he learned his lessons, God had him take the Israelites through the same course.

Traveling toward the truth is what all that traipsing around the desert was about. When we figure out what God wants to teach us, we finally find the way to get out.

Faith is the promised land, and it is inside the souls of true Christians.

It's shifty business sifting through all those shifting sands in the desert, but if you keep moving forward toward God's call on your life, you'll eventually find your way through.

Faith starts in the heart, grows in the heart, melts the heart, and finds the heart of God in everyone.

Reorganizing your religion for lack of better terms just means that you have to let God clean out the creeds clogging your heart and mind. God can put a brand new faith inside of you that will not look anything like the religion you used to display.

Setting sail with the Holy Spirit is a breeze.

Truth is always waiting for you to come home to what is true.

The foundation of all faith is putting the rock solid words of Jesus at the bottom of all your spiritual practices.

Do not worry about losing your religion; if you fill up on religion, you will not have any room for faith.

Religion is a poor substitute for a relationship with God.

Sacraments are man's attempt to put him in right relationship with the church.

Bowing down to religious leaders, or bowing down for religious reasons can give you religious seizures.

Jesus said he came to give us a more abundant life, but many churches have misunderstood that and named themselves after the fact.

I am glad I learned to cry in the desert since there was not anything else to drink.

Better to be in a dry desert with faith than in a cool church with false doctrines.

God has reserved a special place and time to teach you faith, but you will miss the whole offer if you only stay tuned to the religious channel.

Faith comes by hearing the word of God, but futility comes by hearing man's words about God.

Yes, religion makes me angry because it always causes a ruckus. When was the last time you attended a silent service where the Holy Spirit did all the speaking?

I went into the desert to hide out from the deserters of true faith that were dividing the church.

Faith, hope, and love can only spring from one Source, and it is not something you can fashion with your hand.

Grace abounds in the desert for the humble who seek it there.

When religion looks faith in the face, it tries to poke its eyes out. The blind don't like to see anyone looking at them.

Faith is free but religion takes a lot of money to keep it running.

The love of God constrains us, but the love of religion drains us.

Everyone who manages to survive in the desert comes out wiser and stronger.

My church decided I could not attend the conference even though I clearly heard God telling me I should go.

Decisions for planning future programs happens before prayer, otherwise, you can bet some of those programs would never happen.

Study Guide for Discussion Groups

Part One

The scriptural **epigraph** found in Luke 3:4-6 is a prophecy regarding John the Baptist. Read Luke 3:3 and explain how this verse ties in with the prophecy in Isaiah.

What is meant by the phrases every valley shall be filled, every mountain and hill made low, crooked roads shall become straight, and the rough ways smooth? Can you make an application of this to God's work in your life? You may share it with the group if you wish.

In the **Foreword**, what is meant by the term religiosity? Can you find instances in religious practices where this term would be applicable? What was your response to the Author's definition of faith as it contrasts or complements one's religion? What do you consider old-fashioned religion?

What would you derive as the theme of the **Preface?** Do you see a correlation between the desert and your own spiritual journey? Have you had such an experience and how has that strengthened your faith?

On the **Chart of Biblical Desert Incidences** is there a character with whom you can relate based on your relationships and spiritual experience? Please reflect on the connection and explain to the group how God used the experience in your life. Or assign one character per person to read the scriptures and report the details of the incidence back to the group. Share any further observations as found.

What thoughts in the Author's **Introduction** were noteworthy to you?

Chapter 1

A Day of Reckoning for Religion begins with the Author's statement, "We've all been there!" What is that statement in reference to? Why do you think this chapter is titled with the term a day of reckoning?

How did you relate to the descriptive paragraphs about Jesus on pages 3 and 4? Which one statement about him held the most interest to you and why?

On page 6, how do you feel about the author's comments on religious practices that do not have a heart for Jesus at their core? What thought, sentence, or paragraph on this page would you like to elaborate on, either in agreement or disagreement with the author.

After reading the scripture verses on page 11, how would you explain the author's comment, "All deeds of religion done without sincere reverence for God and love for others are actions that begin and end in woe."?

Have you had experience with the author's comment on page 13, "Elevating religious rituals apart from faith and love…becomes our misdirected attempt to earn our way into God's grace"?

Share your experience with religious rituals as they have been a source of blessing and have strengthened your faith in God. (Religious rituals in and of themselves are not bad, but it's the way in which we participate that determines their meaning.) When do our rituals become meaningless?

On page 14, the author ends with her viewpoint that faith in Jesus is the key to a relationship with the Father and says a man's nominal religion is not the key, but rather a lock on the door that no man is ever able to open. What is meant by nominal religion and why would that be considered a lock on the door to keep us from a relationship with God?

Chapter 2

Reconciliation, or "Wreck-of-Conciliation," by Religion has a pretty strong connotation. After reading this chapter, what does the author say is the reconciliation that a religious person could partake of?

Skimming pages 17-20 in the text, what instances of wreck-of-conciliation does the author mention? Notice these are general, not specific instances. Left in general terms, you are free to make your specific application based on your knowledge or experience of problems with the misuse of religion. What connections do you make?

Chapter 3

Why do you think **Shipwrecked Faith ~ Set Sail Again** is the title following the previous chapter? What does it mean to shipwreck your faith according to St. Paul? On page 26, what aspects of our faith if neglected will harm our faith?

Read Genesis 3:1-12, why did Adam hide from God in the garden? Do you think this was the shipwreck of Adam and Eve's faithful relationship with God? Who ultimately caused the shipwreck? (See Genesis 3:14) How could a falsely presented theology cause our faith to falter?

After Reading the Lord's Prayer and the author's concluding remarks on page 30, what foundational Christian principle do we need to apply to keep sailing smoothly in faith?

According to Philippians 2:5-11 and John 7:16-18, what does Jesus demonstrate to us as the course for how to live by faith?

Chapter 4

Repent ~ Return to the Elementary Principle of Faith is not a phrase we hear very often in religious teachings today. However, is it possible to live by faith without first repenting from self-sufficient, or the opposite self-condemning lifestyles? Why?

Today, many of our congregations are focused on a watered down and different gospel. On page 36, do you agree with the author's statement, "The job of the shepherd is to pastor the flock, not pasture a group of followers, organized neatly around a religious corporation."?

Have you seen instances where the gospel of faith in Christ has been altered by the preaching of self-help, purposeful religious lifestyle guidelines, or turned into a formula for how to have your best life experience by adhering to religious ideations. Such teachings idolize our living in the power of positive thinking, or applying scriptural principles to benefit our cause. However, they minimize our living for God to please him in the power of faith and maximize our living to please ourselves in a mindset of willpower.

What are the doctrines found on pages 43-47 that contrast with much of the focus of many modern day preachers and congregations? If there is a different gospel or a different Jesus being promoted among Christian gatherings, could you agree that we need to repent from error and return to the elementary principle of faith that Jesus Christ imparted to his own?

Chapter 5

Do you think the practices in many churches today might have caused a need for **Reorganizing Your Religious Reality?**

What is the basic foundation mentioned on pages 49 and 50 on which we are to build our faith?

After reading the account of the antichrist on page 51, has any profession of religion or religious persons led you or anyone you know away from the practice of a balanced and productive Christian life?

How do the scripture verses on page 51, Matthew 7:15-17, 24:23-24, and 2Thessalonians 2:19-22 tie into the things that are detestable to God listed in Proverbs 6:16 on page 52?

Is there any part of the author's statement on page 52, *"When we embrace Jesus as our Savior, clear our hearts through confession of sin, and ask for God's will to take priority over our carnal nature and earthly goals, God's Holy Spirit comes to reside in us; it's like we are born again."* that you do not understand or agree with? What is it and why do you believe as you do?

On page 53 and 54 what does Jesus instruct will insure that we are living in right relationship to him and our Heavenly Father? How would these instructions be a basis for reorganizing any of our past or present religious reality? What do we gain when we follow God's way for our lives?

Chapter 6

What in the chapter **Hope ~ Help for Healing** was a new concept for your theological perspective?

In the last paragraph on page 61 which continues on page 62, what do Jesus and the Holy Spirit provide through their ministry to humanity?

What specific hope and help for spiritual healing do you need? And which person of the Holy Trinity can you go to in prayer to find healing?

On the last paragraph on page 66 we find the truth of God's healing light. Do you daily consider the power of God's omnipresent light being available to provide hope and help for any healing you may need? Be careful not to start a new doctrine around God's light, just accept the scriptural references as you find them in the context in which they are written. Much of the scripture is allegorical in nature.

Chapter 7

Forsaking Futility or Falling Away ~ Finding Faith in the Desert is a chapter with three themes. What are these three themes and what do they mean for you?

Read Matthew 3 and Luke 3:1-18. What did John preach to the people that opened the way for faith?

John the Baptist was not in the desert because of personal confusion. He was there fulfilling the prophecy in Isaiah 40:3. John preached to people in the desert and many came to faith in that dry place. What encouragement have you found in relationship to spending a dry time spiritually?

In Mark 5:35-36, why does Jesus tell Jairus, the synagogue ruler, to continue to believe even after the horrible news came regarding his daughter? How have we been like Jairus's daughter in the past? What lesson does Jesus teach us when he disregards the mocking laughter of the mourners and goes to the little girl's aid?

Reread the account of Jesus' miracle on page 83 and the first half of page 84. Have you heard the call of Jesus to receive your spiritual salvation, whether it was through a religious experience, or a personal time of prayer and reflection? Have you experienced the presence of God assuring you that you are his child during a time of crisis? When you look back over your life, is there a time when you wanted to live as genuinely as you could through the strength of the indwelling Holy Spirit? Have you experienced a time about which you now marvel over the many ways that God has changed your life? Can you share a testimony of God's redemptive work on your behalf, or in answer to your prayers on behalf of others?

Chapter 8

Traveling Toward Truth opens with the statement, "Don't blame other believers; blame the unbelief!" What is the underlying principle we find stated in this? Can you give an instance from this chapter where Jesus demonstrates this principle in his dealing with people? (Skim pages 89-92.)

How do you feel about the truth of this statement on page 93, *"We have to be committed to our faith in Christ if we are going to give and receive everything meant for us to share with others during our physical life on this earth"*?

In Matthew 25:3-4 what do the wise ones take along with them? This also tells us what we need to pack as we travel toward truth. What is the significance of the lamp oil? Which person of the trinity provides this for our journey toward truth?

Look up the scripture verses listed on page 89. What specific words spoken by the Pharisees proved they were not living in faith, but were bound in unbelief?

On page 90, the author states, "It is the lie in our belief system that keeps us in bondage to the lie of guilt." See page 92 and consider how both the Samaritan woman and Zaccheus were bound in unbelief. What did Jesus do to free them from their bondage to a life of unbelief?

Chapter 9

In this chapter, **Sifting Through Shifting Sands ~ Finding Faith-Filled Friends** what are the shifting sands?

How do you feel about the author's statement on page 100, *"What we do every day of our lives determines whether we are building a rock-solid life, or we are just shifting around buckets of sand."*? Can you describe some daily events as shifting around buckets of sand? Can you elaborate?

Who is the person in your life like Gram who demonstrated what a Christian life should look like in our practice of our Christian faith?

On pages 102-103 what question tells us whether or not we have a real relationship with Jesus Christ?

On page 104, Gram had no regrets for her failures. What did Gram teach about God's forgiveness?

According to the scripture on page 105, what attitudes damage our spirit and hinder many people from accepting the gospel of salvation?

What hindered Peter's return to his walk of faith? How did Jesus restore Peter? (See John 13:36-38 and John 21:15-23.) What shifting sands did Peter immediately start to enter?

Looking at page 107, list at least three things a faith-filled friend can do for you.

According to page 109, what should be our main criteria for finding Christian friends?

Epilogue

After reading the **Epilogue ~ What We Need to Know to Set Sail Again and Serve God** beginning on page 113, what is the most important thing we need to know in order to set sail again and serve God after a faith failure, or shipwrecked faith?

What are the sins of the carnal nature found on pages 114 and 115?

On page 116, according to the author what are virtues and what happens to our faith during testing?

On page 117, how was Jesus different from the religious leaders of his day?

After reading page 118, what are some of the problems religiosity causes for us?

Why is it important for us to know sound doctrine, beware of false prophets and teachers, and not to become entangled in legalistic traditions?

What happens to us when we embrace false prophets and teachers, and legalistic traditions instead of guarding our faith? How could these issues cause us to sin and render our faith ineffective?

Close your discussion group with a reading of Matthew 5:1-11 and prayer for each member of the group to grow closer to Jesus.

WRITE A PRAYER PAGE

(Please feel free to use this page to write what's
on your heart as a prayer before God.)

CPSIA information can be obtained
at www.ICGtesting.com
Printed in the USA
LVOW03s0233290118
564405LV00001B/58/P

9 781449 710866